THE BUSKERS

THE BUSKERS

*A History of
Street Entertainment*

DAVID COHEN
& BEN GREENWOOD

DAVID & CHARLES
Newton Abbot   London   North Pomfret (Vt)

British Library Cataloguing in Publication Data

Cohen, David
  The buskers.
  1. Street music and musicians – History
  2. Street theatre – History
  I. Title   II. Greenwood, Ben
  790.2   PN1581

  ISBN 0 7153 8026 5

Library of Congress Catalog Card Number: 80-85500

Typeset by Typesetters (Birmingham) Ltd
Smethwick, Warley, West Midlands
and printed in Great Britain
by Biddles Limited, Guildford, Surrey
for David & Charles (Publishers) Limited
Brunel House   Newton Abbot   Devon

Published in the United States of America
by David & Charles Inc
North Pomfret   Vermont 05053   USA

CONTENTS

LIST OF ILLUSTRATIONS

Plates

Figures

To Nicola and Lucy

INTRODUCTION

Our research into this subject began as a result of a concern with circumstances which we find in today's town life. We seem to live in a society which shows little interest in caring for its street environment. If it is true that the behaviour of people is substantially a response to the environment in which they live, then certainly those responsible for what is built should take a critical look at themselves and at the worth of their contribution to communities. Buildings which reflect the ego of designers or which are experimental at the expense of everyday users create the climate for unhappy communities, and there seems to be no shortage of discontent in our towns and cities today. Given the importance of buildings and their relationship to one another, perhaps it can also be argued that too much emphasis is placed on the actual buildings, and not enough on the spaces between them where people meet. Thus there is doubt about both the atmosphere created by the buildings and the spaces they define. At street level, the carefully orchestrated arrangements of potted plants which we find in our towns seem to do little more than attract vandals, and for the more caring members of our society one wonders how much the predictable layout of these artefacts really adds to the joy of being in a place. All seems designed to hurry us in and out: the prospect of surprise or romantic association of any kind seems to be totally beyond the wit of the organisers of our environment.

In street entertainment we are dealing with a much undervalued element of town life. We do not claim that the presence of street entertainers is a counter measure against those bent on trouble; pickpockets, vandals and tramps seem to feature in every generation of urban society and it would be naïve to think that this will change in the future.

We hope that this book will interest and fascinate the reader in a subject which in its own right has surprised us with the richness of its history, showing beyond doubt that today's street entertainer can identify with generations of artists who in their different ways have made their own unorthodox contributions to street life.

We have enjoyed finding characters of bygone years and would like to feel that the book will inspire people to take a more enlightened and generous attitude towards today's travelling exhibitionists and entertainers. Many do not perform very well, but as with all trades and professions, those who are not good enough will not be tolerated by the public. Those who are will survive, and given the appreciation of the towns they visit, will, we hope, become the historical characters of future books.

David Cohen 1981

THE MINSTREL'S FATE
IS TO BE A WANDERER

This book is about individualists. History tends to concentrate on the development of societies, or on the powerful individuals who controlled the lives of their members. It is our task to trace a tradition of people who chose to defy class structure, and take their chances on the roads and streets. The position of the performer in society has always been a dubious one, and that of his itinerant brother even more precarious. The taste among wealthy people for 'slumming it' is an age-old one, and the establishment has always tended to patronise privately while publicly condemning popular forms of amusement. In Ancient Rome, for example, it was against the law for anyone of senatorial or equestrian rank publicly to consort with professional actors or musicians, but in the early Empire, both Caligula and Nero actually performed in public. Centuries later the novelist Henry Fielding, whose magistracy at Bow Street did much towards cleaning up London crime, ran a theatrical booth for nine years at the annual hot-bed of low life Bartholomew Fair, at a period when the fair was patronised by the Prince of Wales, later George II.

The distinction between itinerant and street performers is, for our purposes, largely redundant. The terms are obviously not synonymous, but there is a fair amount of overlap, and it is often a matter of environment. Street life is a characteristic of cities and towns, while a wider horizon shows us itinerants, but the characters are essentially the same.

The fall of the Roman Empire and the turmoil of the Dark Ages prevent us from claiming a tradition, in the strictest sense, of street life, but the fact that certain characteristics re-emerge in our modern cities suggests that street entertaining is one of those features that tend to crop up, like usury, prostitution, crime and poverty, wherever settlements develop into cities.

The evidence of street entertainment in Rome is scarce. Educated Romans were worlds apart from their plebeian countrymen, and writers did not consider busking a subject worthy of notice, so we have to glean what we can from whatever sources are available. Martial gives us an interesting picture of first-century Rome in his epigrams:

> On this side the money-changer idly rattles on his dirty table Nero's coins, on that the hammerer of Spanish gold dust beats his well-worn stone with burnished mallet; and Bellona's raving throng does not rest, nor the canting ship-wrecked seaman with his swathed body (feigning amputation) . . .[1]

The singing sailor is the earliest example of the lowest form of street entertainment, that of using music, or often simply noise, to draw attention to misfortune. He reappears often, in particular in London at the time of the Napoleonic Wars, but we are not so cynical as to suggest that he is always a phoney on the make.

Dio Chrysostom, who was born in Bithynia in AD 40, gives us another glimpse, from roughly the same period, of the intense activity that took place in the streets and public places. He describes tutors of the flute, the harp, painting, and even reading and writing, teaching their pupils in the open air, and goes on to mention performers:

> And I remember once seeing, while walking through the Hippodrome, many people on one spot and each one doing something different; one playing the flute, another dancing, another doing a juggler's trick, another reading a poem aloud, another singing and another telling some story or myth.[2]

Dio was from Prusa in Bithynia, but he spent some time in Rome during the reign of Vespasian (AD 69–79). He was expelled by Domitian, but returned under Nerva and Trajan. There is no indication here whether he is referring to Rome or to Prusa, but Rome was the capital of the empire, and by that time 'Roman' could refer to cities in Italy, Asia Minor, and even Gaul.

Plate 1 Street performers acting Menander's *Theophorumene*, by
Dioscourides of Samos, first century AD

The finest evidence of street entertainment is in a mosaic by
Dioscourides of Samos, possibly of the first century, now in the
Museum of Naples (*see* Plate 1). It has been matched with a much
inferior, but named, third-century copy, and the group has been
recognised as taking part in a pantomimic representation of
Menander's *Theophorumene*, Act 5. The liberal arts were much
more unified in Ancient Rome than they are today, and music
was just one of the capabilities of the all-round pantomime actor.

We know, then, that Rome and her cities had street
performers. The question now is how or why they got there.

The origins of Roman society are deeply rooted in agrarian tradition, and we look to the *Ludi Compitales*, or Compitalian Games, as a possible key. In the countryside, shrines developed at crossroads, sacred to the *Lares Compitales*, the gods of the crossroads. A festival developed to worship these gods, situated between the Saturnalia (17 December) and 5 January. This was a time of resting and celebration for agricultural workers. These agricultural festivals were the origin of the Roman songs of abuse, which developed into bitter personal attacks, and in the later Republic were sung outside the houses of individuals, or at public assemblies. The songs originated in the *fescennina*. At the early festivals the farming ancestors of the Romans would entertain themselves by being rude to each other in verse. The songs were a form of raillery that invited reply, and were all in good fun. The name derives from an Italian town, Fescennia, but the custom was popular all over Italy. Horace tells us how this simple form of merry-making became a little too abusive:

> '. . . the Fescennine licentiousness poured forth its rustic taunts in alternative stanzas; and this liberty, received down through revolving years, sported pleasingly; till at length the bitter raillery began to be turned into open rage, and threatened with impunity to stalk through reputable families. They, who suffered from its bloody tooth, smarted with the pain; the unhurt likewise were concerned for the common condition: further also, a law and penalty were enacted which forbade that any one should be stigmatised in lampoon.[3]

The laws of the Twelve Tables were compiled in 451 BC, sixty-one years after the expulsion of the kings by the Roman people. These laws included the prohibition of the singing or composing of *libelli famosi*, libellous pamphlets or songs (*libellus* means 'small book'). The imposition of the death penalty, however, was not enough to stem an urge germane to the Italian peoples, and abusive songs of varying intensities continued.

In urban Rome, the *compita*, or crossroads in areas of housing, became meeting places for the lower classes, including slaves. They still had their *lares*, and the religious significance was not lost. Artisans' guilds, *collegia compitalicia*, developed, quasi-

religious organisations of working men, whose festivals became
the *Ludi Compitales*. The importance of drama in religious ritual
will be discussed later on. The festivals took place in the streets,
and were the scene of entertainments, planned and spontaneous,
from troupes of mime artists, solo musicians and street poets.
The *compita* became a focal point for the common people, and the
natural venue for itinerant performers, who would visit and play
not only at festivals, but at any time.

The satirical street poets have left the most evidence behind
them, partly because they managed to creep into the literature of
the Latin language. The playwright Plautus (*c.* 250–184 BC)
gives an indication of what could be expected in his play *Mercator*.
Demipho, a lecherous old man, says that he dares not allow his
son to present a beautiful slavegirl to his mother.[4] It would
attract singers outside their house, and would lead to the
suspicion that Demipho, supposedly a respectable man, was
procuring. The singers at this level were a sort of immediate
Private Eye. If a well-known person did anything doubtful, he
would be liable to find a singer outside his door, broadcasting the
facts to the general public. The lowly have always taken a great
delight in laughing at the foibles and weaknesses of the great,
and this singing could be described as a kind of oral graffiti. It
could be the spontaneous reaction of the jealous poor, but it
could also be a more calculated attempt by an enemy to publicly
humiliate a respectable figure. Songs were sometimes composed
by people who desired to remain anonymous, and were sung by
hired singers. Other composers did not remain anonymous, as
the laws of the Twelve Tables had fallen into disuse in the later
Republic, but they possibly considered themselves too noble to
get their feet dirty.

At this point we find the poet Catullus, many of whose songs
were abusive in the extreme. He was born in 87 BC at Verona, a
member of the provincial élite. He came to Rome as a young
man of easy circumstances, and became part of a circle of young
men known as the New Poets. This group included Calvus,
Cinna, Cornificius, Valerius Cato, Furius Bibaculus, and
Ticidas, but Catullus was the most illustrious. They used to
meet and experiment in new poetical techniques and metres. The

highest form of literature of the time was considered to be historical epic, and had always been ever since the Romans became aware of Homer. Latin was still to realise its climax in this genre with the *Aeneid* of Virgil, who was about seventeen years younger than Catullus, but the literature of the New Poets was something quite different to this. They wrote short, clever, personal poems that lived off and alluded to the gossip of the time. Catullus created a literary form out of a tradition that was as old as Rome. Simply because he was a poet, and his poems have come down to us, does not place him apart from other composers of songs of abuse. His poems were written to be heard by the targets of his wit, and also by everybody else, and they were no less obscene, insulting or direct than any piece of doggerel sung by the mob outside the house of an unpopular official. Number 41 is one of the milder ones:

> Just now Ameana, that worn-out
> Tart with the ugly turned-up snout
> Who goes around with you-know-who
> The Formian bankrupt who's run through
> His fortune—asked me, if you please,
> For a cool ten thousand sesterces.
> Her guardians or her next-of-kin
> Should call her friends and doctors in,
> She's mad, and since she never faces
> Mirrors, can't see how bad her case is.[5]

One of Catullus' main objectives was to show off his own wit at the public expense of others, an innocuous one compared to the aims of some of the political figures of the late Republic, who used street singers as part of their propaganda machines. One of these was Publius Clodius, a powerful man in the power struggles at the end of the Republic. In 58 BC he was elected a tribune through the help of Julius Caesar, who, as Pontifex Maximus, head of the Roman religion, sanctioned Clodius' adoption into a plebeian family (an aristocrat could not become tribune). Clodius understood well the importance of the *compita* and, although he appeared to side with the triumvirate of Caesar, Pompey and Crassus against the Senate, he passed a number of measures that increased his own popularity and strength among the people. In 64 BC the Senate had abolished the *collegia compitalicia*, but Clodius reversed this, and organised and armed them into what were virtually his own troops. He also made the doles of cheap corn absolutely free, and increased the number of recipients. In 57 he quarrelled with Pompey, who was afraid to leave his own house for months, so complete was Clodius' control of the streets. The triumvirate got Titus Annius Milo, another tribune, to organise rival bands of street thugs and gladiators, to contest Clodius' superiority. As a result of this in 56 Clodius prosecuted Milo on a charge of violence. His supporters crowded into the courts, and shouted and sang abuse at Pompey, who was defending Milo. When Clodius came to make his speech, he got similar treatment, and insulting epigrams about him and his allegedly immoral sister Clodia so put him off that Pompey won. Mob rule had taken over from simple verbal attack on the streets, though, and when in 52 Milo had Clodius murdered, the enraged mob burned the Senate house and the nearby Porcian basilica.

Everybody knows the figure who seized power out of this turmoil. Julius Caesar ruled Rome for four years after defeating Pompey in 48. Caesar was the most powerful man in Rome, partly because of his wealth, and partly because of the loyalty of his veteran legions from the Gallic campaigns. But he underestimated the importance of public opinion. He abolished once more the *collegia compitalicia*, just one of the moves that led people to see him as tyrant. When he appointed new senators, a song went round every street corner mocking him:

> Caesar led the Gauls to triumph,
>   Led them uphill, led them down,
> To the Senate House he took them,
>   Once the glory of our town.
> 'Pull those breeches off,' he shouted,
>   'Change into a purple gown.'[6]

Perhaps he should have listened to the voice of public opinion more closely. In 44 he was murdered by men who wanted to free Rome from a despot.

The man who, at the Battle of Actium in 31, finally ended the struggle was Octavius. He was more aware of the importance of public opinion than his uncle had been, and gave himself the title of *princeps*, or first member of the state. He later became known as Augustus. He was frequently the subject of lampoons, often directed against his personal life, but he chose to argue against their content rather than ban them. It was not until very near the end of his reign, in AD 12, that he found cause to revive the laws of the Twelve Tables concerning *libelli famosi*. A friend of his, Cassius Severus, had defamed distinguished men and women with his writings to such a degree of abusiveness that Augustus felt compelled to take action. He ordered the *aediles*, public officers, to search Rome for any such publications, and burn what they found. The death penalty for producing, or even possessing, such material was revived. Apart from this, Augustus' reign was not an authoritarian one. He revived the *Ludi Compitales*, not as a means of gaining popularity, but because he believed they had a genuine place in the traditional religion of Rome. The *collegia compitalicia* were also revived, but as organised bodies responsible for the regulation of crafts, and also as part of the worship of the crossroad gods. He was personally responsible for the financing of many games and festivals.

Satirical songs were also part of Roman life in a less politically exploitable way. It became the custom at funerals to sing songs about the deceased, drawing attention to his or her characteristics. These would scarcely have been as defamatory and bitter as those with political or personal malicious intent, because their subjects had passed beyond attack and, moreover, could hardly reply to their accusations. But they served to remember the person for what he or she had been, faults and all. For example, Vespasian had a reputation for meanness. In his lifetime he rebuilt the stage at the Theatre of Marcellus, and at its dedication gave four hundred thousand sesterces to Apelles the tragic actor, two hundred thousand each to Terpnus and Diodorus the lyre players, and smaller sums to other performers. Despite this and other acts of generosity, his reputation went with him to the grave:

And when he died, the famous comedian Favor, who had been chosen to wear his funeral mask in the procession and give the customary imitations of his gestures and words, shouted to the procurators: 'Hey, how much will all this cost?' 'A hundred thousand,' they answered. 'Then I'll take a thousand down, and you can just pitch me into the Tiber.'[7]

The history of Roman drama is well documented, and is worth relating briefly, not only because we know it was performed in the streets, but also because some of its characteristics reappear in medieval Europe. Livy, writing around 26 BC, tells us that the first scenic entertainments were introduced to appease the gods during a pestilence in 364 BC: 'players who had been brought in from Etruria danced to the strains of the flautist and performed not ungraceful evolutions in the Tuscan fashion'.[8] The performers were called *histriones*, from the Etruscan word *ister*, meaning 'player', and the term came to mean all professional pantomime or mime players.

The next development in pantomime came from Livius Andronicus, who first came to Rome in 272 BC. He was the first to use a narrative plot, and it is said that his voice suffered so much from singing encores that he engaged a singer, while himself concentrating on the art of gesture. The *pantomimus* wore a mask, and danced silently to the theme sung by the *chorus* accompanied by flute. The *chorus* kept time by tapping his foot, wearing a *scabellum*, or wooden sole. The pantomime reached the height of its development in the reign of Augustus (27 BC–AD 14), with the dancers Bathyllus, Pylades, and Hylas. Despite the profession's lack of respectability, they were universally popular, and their rivalry caused outbreaks of violence which compelled the Senate to impose laws. Senators were not allowed into the houses of *pantomimi*, and knights were forbidden to consort with them publicly, or to watch their performances, except in the theatre. The top performers were social interlopers, comparable in fame, notoriety, and popularity to Mick Jagger, and one of them, Mnester, was the Emperor Caligula's favourite, with whom he had a homosexual relationship.[9] The best of them were artists of the highest note, taking their themes from the tragedies of Sophocles and Euripides. Lucian, in his *Saltatio*, written about AD 165, describes the response of a dancer of Nero's day to the scornful challenge of Demetrius the Cynic:

> Enjoining silence upon the stampers and flute players and upon the chorus itself, quite unsupported, he danced the amours of Aphrodite and Ares, Helius rattling, Hephaestus buying his plot and trapping both of them with his entangling bonds, the gods who came in on them, portrayed individually, Aphrodite ashamed, Ares seeking cover and begging for mercy, and everything that belongs to this story, in such wise that Demetrius was delighted beyond measure with what was taking place and paid the highest possible tribute to the dancer; he raised his voice and shouted at the top of his lungs: 'I hear the story that you are acting man, I do not just see it; you seem to me to be talking with your very hands.'[10]

Distinct from the cultured pantomine, mime was for those with coarser tastes. It aped foolish and obscene situations with gesture and mimicry, and little dialogue. Masks were not worn, and grimaces were part of the means of expression. The Greek word *mimos* means 'one who makes grimaces'. During the early Republic when religious ritual was still meaningful, it was the custom during festivals to perform crude comedies from the backs of wagons. The rites of Bacchus were particularly associated with the dramatic arts, and in 186 BC the Bacchanalia were suppressed because it was feared that the noise of drums, cymbals and voices drowned the cries of sufferers at perverted orgies and murders. The Bacchic rites were the origin of the stage phallus that became a characteristic of the mimes.

As Rome grew more urban, performances retained their connection with festivals, but the religious significance was superceded by the political expedient of keeping the crowd happy. During the Empire, mime took over from Atellan plays as a form of light relief after tragedies. These Atellan plays were farces, traditionally performed by free-born Romans without social stigma. Various stock character types developed, Maccus the clown, Buccones the babbler, and Simus the baboon, for example. These were gradually absorbed by the mimes, acted by *histriones*. During the first two centuries AD the most popular mime was Catullus' *Laureolus*, in which a highwayman is crucified. The Emperor Domitian (c. AD 81–96) increased his popularity by allowing condemned prisoners to be executed as part of the act. The decline of democracy seemed to coincide with a coarsening of the tastes of the Roman people. During the Republic, Greek tragedy and comedy had been popular, but these were superceded by mime and pantomine. Pompey's theatre, built in 55 BC, seated 27,000, but that was negligible compared to the 255,000 capacity of the Circus Maximus in which gladiators fought to the death. It was essential for Emperors to retain their popularity. Rome had 150,000 people kept idle at state expense, and their minds had to be diverted away from politics. In Claudius' day (AD 41–54) there were 159 holidays in a year, not to speak of various quadrennial cycles, and games decreed by Caesar as triumphs. Entertainment, along with free food, was a means of political control, and it is not surprising that no regime attempted to ban street performances.

In AD 410 Rome was sacked by Alaric. People tend to think of the Dark Ages as completely obliterating Roman culture. This is of course too simple a view. The barbarians disliked theatre, but liked *mimi*, with their associated talents of tumbling, juggling and tight-rope walking. In 448 Attila entertained ambassadors from the Eastern Roman Empire, and the entertainment included a Teutonic bard, or *scop*, and Moorish and Scythian buffoons (by that time Roman culture had influenced most of the Mediterranean and Asia Minor, and the buffoons were essentially of the Roman tradition). At the start of the sixth century the Ostrogoth Theodoric found it necessary to allow dramatic spectacles to keep the native population happy. In 533 Justinian, Emperor in the East, reconquered Rome, and it was not until 568, and the advent of the Lombards, that the theatres were finally closed, and the *histriones* turned out onto the road. Nineteenth-century historians like to suggest that troupes of mimers, pantomimers and musicians tramped around Europe for centuries, until their re-emergence in Renaissance Italy. Unfortunately, information fails us at this point, but certain stylistic similarities were preserved, which will be examined in a later chapter.

The Teutonic barbarians had their own musicians, who were regarded as equal to noblemen. The word *scop* is from the verb *skapan*, 'to make', and, as in Greek, is virtually synonymous with 'poet', a term of honour. They were traditionally wanderers, and were responsible for spreading the fame of Germanic heroes and kings all over Europe. Leofric, Bishop of Exeter 1046–72, made a collection of Old English poems, known as the Exeter Book, and amongst these is *Widsith* or *The Far-Traveller*, thought to have been composed in seventh-century Mercia. The poem relates the journey of Widsith, a *scop* from the Myrging tribe of Germany, who accompanies Ealhild, a Lombard princess, to the court of Eormanric the Goth, her future husband. But Ealhild was sister of King Aelfwine, who died in 573, about two hundred years after the death of Eormanric. Widsith names sixty-one great men, whom he claims to have visited, who have been proved to date from the third, fourth, fifth and sixth centuries AD. The poem is a catalogue of kings and heroes from the pre-Christian, heroic period of Germanic expansion over Europe, and listeners would have recognised the names from other heroic poems. The story told may be impossible, but it tells us a lot about the function of the *scop*, spreading throughout Europe the stories of Germanic heroes, and it also shows that he was a figure welcomed by kings and noblemen. Widsith says that Eormanric gave him a ring made of six hundred shillings' worth of pure gold. The end of the poem hints that such largesse was likely to come from a king who desired his fame to be spread abroad:

The makar's wierd is to be a wanderer:[11]
the poets of mankind go through the many countries,
speak their needs, say their thanks.
Always they meet with someone, in the south lands or the north,
who understands their art, an open handed man
who would not have his fame fail among the guard
nor rest from an earl's deeds before the end cuts off
light and life together.
    Lasting honour shall be his,˙
a name that shall never die beneath the heavens.[12]

Old English poetry is full of wanderers and exiles. The *scop* was dependent on a lord's generosity, which could not be counted on as permanent, and his changing fortunes may have been one reason for his travelling life. *Deor*, written in eighth-century Wessex, is the story of an exiled *scop*, and illustrates the insecurity of a life based on patronage:

> . . . in the hall of the Heodenings I held long the makarship,
> lived dear to my prince, Deor my name;
> many winters I held this happy place
> and my lord was kind. Then came Heorrenda,
> whose lays were skilful; the lord of fighting-men
> settled on him the estate bestowed once on me.[13]

By the time these poems were written, Europe had undergone another conquest of a more permanent and comprehensive nature. Charlemagne was King of the Franks, originally a tribe of northern barbarians, but in 813 he died as Holy Roman Emperor. The combination of Empire and Papacy in a temporal and spiritual kingdom called Christendom was just the germ of an idea, but it was beginning to grow. The Church was becoming a unifying power in Europe, and it was also becoming a powerful censor of behaviour. Its language was Latin, and the existence of a language understood throughout Europe by educated men meant that the development of a single code of conduct could be attempted. In the eighth century Alcuin, Charlemagne's adviser, wrote to Higbald, an English bishop, warning him of the moral dangers of allowing licence to *ioculatores*. The blanket term indicates that in the eyes of the Church there was no difference between Germanic bards or Romanic buffoons. By that time, of course, the mingling of races had caused a fusion of talents. Anglo-Saxon illuminated manuscripts show *gleomen*, or *gleemen*, who were journeymen entertainers, singers and tumblers, without the exalted position of the *scop*. Some of the postures of the tumblers show that they have learned a trick or two from the *mimi*. In 789 the Church forbade its bishops, abbots and abbesses to keep *ioculatores*, and in 802 all clergymen were ordered to refrain from idle amusement. At the Council of Tours in the year of his death, Charlemagne confirmed these prohibitions. And yet he himself kept minstrels at court, and collected the heroic songs of his ancestors. Here we have the embryo of the medieval tradition of minstrelsy. Those who were favoured with patronage could travel with their lord's protection, while those without were virtually outlaws. It is not being suggested that Charlemagne was a hypocrite because he liked music, or that any market-place buffoon had the same artistic merit as the minstrel who wrote and sang the *Song of Roland*, but history repeatedly shows us the men in power trying to deprive the common people of amusement, while enjoying themselves as they pleased. Charlemagne's son, Louis the Pious, was more austere than his father, and turned the minstrels out of court. He also issued a decree forbidding dances, songs, and tales in public places and at crossroads on Sundays. This may appear as an attempt to keep the Sabbath pure from scurrility. It may also have stemmed from a desire to stamp out all remains of the old pagan religion latent in the habits of the common folk. But as all the common people worked for the rest of the week, it in fact meant a complete prohibition of their fun. Louis may seem to be more consistent than his father by turning out his own minstrels, but he was simply a religious bigot, whose piety was the cause of many painful deaths. He excluded *histriones* and *scurrae*, which included all entertainers without noble protection, from the privilege of justice, making them outlaws legally as well as effectually.

Church and aristocracy conspired to ensure that in the feudal pyramid the peasants stayed at the bottom of the pile. By making dissent a sin against God's great scheme, the Church gave kings and nobles the moral muscle to oppress. Wandering minstrels were not only entertainers and newscasters; they also spread ideas, different ideas from those traditionally disseminated from the pulpit. It is ridiculous to suppose that all lords were fair-minded and moral leaders, while all itinerant entertainers were lewd and immoral, likely to lead innocent audiences to Hell, but this is what the Church wanted people to believe, and much of the clerical opposition to *ioculatores* was for political reasons. The political significance of the itinerant entertainer will be an underlying theme of the ensuing chapters.

Notes to Chapter 1

1 Martial, *Epigrams*, XII, LVII.
2 Dio Chrysostom, 20, 9–10.
3 Horace, *Epistles*, II, 1, 139.
4 Plautus, *Mercator*, Act II, Scene IV.
5 Catullus, *Poems*, 41.
6 Suetonius, *Julius Caesar*, 80.
7 Suetonius, *Vespasian*, 19.
8 Livy, *History of Rome*, Book VII.
9 Caligula reigned AD 37–41.
10 Lucian, *De Saltatio*, 63.
11 'makar's wierd': poet's destiny.
12 From *The Earliest English Poems*, translated by Michael Alexander (1977), p. 42.
13 Ibid., p. 37.

2

GOLIARDS
AND TROUBADOURS

Goliard is a name loosely applied to a type of itinerant singing lower clergyman of the early Middle Ages. It was the pattern for most scholars to travel about Europe, as one seat of learning held a very different idea from another. Printing had not been invented, and literature was far from universal. The contents of the libraries of various monasteries and universities differed sufficiently to encourage true scholars to abandon the settled life and take to the roads. As ordained clerics, their interests should have been solely in Christian literature, but on their travels many of them discovered the ancient classics. These heathen writers were considered by the Church to be mortal to the soul, and most deadly of all was poetry. So the Church was angered when its lower members started to produce poetry. A manuscript, known as the *Cambridge Songs*, is thought to be the song-book of an unknown *clericus vagabundus*. It was most probably copied at the monastery of St Augustine at Canterbury from an original, thought to have been acquired by an Englishman travelling in the middle and lower Rhine areas in the mid eleventh century. The forty-seven songs are nearly all in Latin. Of these, nine are love songs, demonstrating an apprenticeship to the archfiend Ovid.

The name goliard comes from an imaginary Bishop Golias, a satirical personification of many of the vices within the Church. Some confusion has grown up in the myth surrounding Golias, and his author, Walter Mapes. Mapes was an English priest, favourite of Henry II, canon of Salisbury and St Paul's, and praecentor of Lincoln, who died in 1210. He wrote the *Confessio Goliae*, or *The Confession of Golias*, as a satirical attack on the abuses of higher clergymen, including corruption, worldliness, and carnality. He is also wrongly credited with having written a

Latin drinking ode, which spread the reputation of the goliards, and of Mapes himself, through Europe:

> I'm fixed; I'll in some tavern lie
>   When I return to dust;
> And have the bottle at my mouth,
>   To moisten my dry crust:
> That the choice spirits of the skies
>   (Who know my soul is mellow)
> May say, Ye gods, propitious smile
> Here comes an honest fellow.[1]

The imitation in English is an eighteenth-century one, and sacrifices accuracy to rhyme and metre, but conveys the impiety well enough. This is the other side of the goliards' image. The system of monastic hospitality was ripe for exploitation. The Church was full of barely educated men, not the slightest bit interested in saving souls, but perfectly happy to live off the sedentary monks, moving from place to place after a few days' rest in each. It seems that Golias became for them a literal figurehead for loose living in a way that the sober Mapes had never intended. As ever, it is impossible to know where to draw the line dividing the drunken lechers from the serious itinerant scholars. Many of the finest scholars were also inclined towards drinking and womanising. It is also true that the satirical message behind the *Confessio Goliae* would not have been lost on them. It was well known that laxity of morals went through the clergy all the way up to the Pope. One of the main reasons why the goliards were frowned upon was that they publicised this immorality by singing about their superiors in taverns, and even in some instances on the streets. In 1289 the Statuta Synodalia Cadurcensis, Rutherensis, et Tutelensis Ecclesiarum decreed that no clerk was to be a jongleur,[2] a goliard, or a buffoon. Not much is heard of goliards after that date, but the word passed into the language, ceasing to have an exclusively clerical application. In the *Prologue* to the *Canterbury Tales*, written in the late fourteenth century, Chaucer tells us of the Miller:

> He was a jangler, and a goliardeis,
> And that was most of sinne and harlotries.[3]

It is worth noting that *The Miller's Tale* is one of the most obscene of all the *Canterbury Tales*, and represents the common vernacular tradition so strongly contrasting with the courtly and antiquated tradition of the Knight and his tale.

This brings us conveniently to a courtly and chivalric tradition that lies behind a popular misconception. Most people nowadays think of troubadours simply as medieval wandering minstrels, whereas the name belongs to a flowering of culture belonging to twelfth-century Provence, southern France, and northern Spain. This area was very much prone to Moorish influences, and it is in Moorish Spain that the troubadour tradition has its origins. In the eleventh century the Moors were far more civilised than their Christian neighbours, and a tradition of music and sung poetry had developed quite independently of North Africa, where poetry was spoken only, and music forbidden by the Koran. Musical instruments such as the lyre, lute, or dulcimer, all of

Figure 1 From a thirteenth-century
French painting

eastern origin, would be kept at houses of repute, in case the household should be favoured by the visit of a minstrel. Certain verse forms developed, which are also recognisable in eleventh-century Provençal folk songs, as well as in troubadour poetry. The *tenson*, for example, is a sort of verbal duel between two contending voices, and is characteristic of both Muslim and troubadour. The Moors and the Christians lived in harmony for three centuries—until the twelfth century when Alfonso VIII of Aragon's Burgundian wife brought religious fanaticism with her—and during that period there was much cultural inter-change, the ruder northerners adopting many of the ways of the civilised Moors. There was fighting, of course, but this was in the nature of feuding lords, as happened constantly in Christian Europe. In one of these feuds in 1064 King Sancho-Ramiro of Aragon and Guilhelm VI of Poitiers and VIII of Aquitaine captured Barbastro, and their booty included many accomplished Moorish singers. In 1094 Guilhelm's son, Guilhelm IX, came to Spain to marry Sancho-Ramiro's widow Philippa. He was the first recorded troubadour.

Troubadour is the Languedoc word for 'finder' or 'inventor', and is comparable to the Teutonic *scop*. A troubadour was essentially a knight who wrote poetry and music. He was expected to travel around the country, visiting and entertaining courts. He was an honoured guest, and much welcomed. Communities could easily become isolated in the days when travel was dangerous and telecommunication non-existent, and a troubadour was responsible for spreading news as well as saving people from the ennui of court life. He would bring with him several jongleurs, professional musicians, who would perform his pieces. The highlight of the visit would be when the troubadour himself performed.

The crusades were another factor that opened Oriental culture to Europe. Guilhelm IX returned from the first crusade in 1102 and, according to Ordericus Vitalis, 'sang before the princes and the great assemblies of the Christians, of the miseries of his captivity among the Saracens, using rhymed verse jovially modulated'.[4] Guilhelm was the grandfather of the most famous patron of troubadours, Eleanor of Aquitaine. Eleanor, after divorcing Louis VII of France, whom she found too austere, set up her own sovereign court in Bordeaux, which became a centre of culture to which many troubadours went. In 1154 she went to England to be crowned Henry II's queen, and took her court of patronage with her. Her son, Richard Coeur-de-Lyon, was also a troubadour. There are two of Richard's poems extant, one a complaint written in prison, where he was held by the Duke of Austria while trying to return from the Holy Land. The story of his release is a well-known one. His jongleur, Blondel, is supposed to have discovered his whereabouts by singing one half of a *tenson* outside a castle, and hearing the reply sung by the imprisoned composer within. Unfortunately, it is not considered to be a true story. Richard was a paradigm of chivalry. He combined the courtly talents of music and poetry, essential to the perfect knight, with courage and prowess in war, as well as a zealous devotion to the Cross. He also exemplified the hypocrisy behind the ideal, however, when he broke his word to his Muslim opponent in a truce, and slaughtered four thousand prisoners.

The other great dynasty of troubadours was that of Raimon Berengar, Count of Barcelona. In 1112 he married the heiress of Provence, and opened the way for Hispano–Moorish culture. Provençal became the language of the troubadours, and Provence the most civilised country in Europe. Raimon's grandson was Alfonso II of Aragon, who reigned 1162–96, and Provence remained an Aragonese fief until 1213. Alfonso and his son Pedro II were both troubadours themselves, and held courts of patronage. Pedro, described as 'the flower of courtesy, the green leaf of delight, the fruit of noble deeds',[5] was killed in 1213 trying to resist a Papal crusade against the troubadours. The crusade will be mentioned later.

Under the patronage of kings, queens and lords, many lesser men became troubadours. Some took to the road as a remedy for lost fortunes, such as Gaucelm Faidit, who lost everything he owned at dice. Others were of humble origin, and trained as jongleurs, but excelled their masters. Uc de Saint-Syr, himself a troubadour, wrote short biographies of many of these less powerful men. He tells us that Perdigon was the son of a fisherman, who by his own skill attracted the notice of the Dauphin of Auvergne, and was made a knight, with estates of his own. The story of Bernart de Ventadorn is even more remarkable. His father was a stoker at the castle of Ventadorn, in Limousin, but the Viscount of Ventadorn brought him up as a musician. The songs he wrote were mainly in favour of the Viscountess, and eventually the Viscount expelled him in a fit of jealousy. He came to Eleanor's court at Bordeaux, where he was well received by the young, romantic Duchess. Eleanor is supposed to have fallen in love with this stoker's son, and even taken him to England when she married Henry. Bernart's verse is some of the best existing troubadour poetry, and has been compared to Wordsworth's in its freshness, and its love of the country, without stepping outside the conventions of its genre. We quote in Provençal, to convey the rhythms of the verse:

> Quant vey la lauzeta mover
> De joi sas alas contral rai,
> que s'oblida e.s laissa cazer
> per la doussor qu' al cor li vai,
> ai! tan grans enveia m'en ve
> de cui qu'en veya jauzion.
> meravilhas ai, quar desse
> lo cor de dezirier nom fon.

In English:

> When I see the lark flutter
> with joy towards the sun,
> and forget himself and sing
> for the sweetness that comes to his heart;
> alas, such envy comes upon me
> of all that I see rejoicing,
> I wonder that forthwith
> my heart does not melt with desire.[6]

Love was one of the favourite subjects of the troubadours, but it was a courtly unreal love that was far removed from real experience. Uc de Saint-Syr's biography of Jaufre Rudel of Blaia exemplifies the troubadour's hopeless, idealistic love. He is said to have fallen desperately in love with the Countess of Tripoli simply from her reputation, and spent a long time writing desperate songs in her honour. He eventually made the long journey to Tripoli just to see her, but fell as if dead as the ship approached port. He was carried ashore, and the Countess immediately visited him. He died in her arms, happy at having finally seen the object of his desire, and she became a nun for grief. The story has not been authenticated, but it demonstrates how divorced from real life the ideals of chivalry were.

One of the most attractive characters was Peire Vidal, and he also demonstrated certain odd behaviour on falling in love with a lady called Loba (She-Wolf) of Penautier:

> Now, the Loba was of Carcassonne and Peire Vidal made himself to be called Lop (Wolf) for love of her, bearing a wolf on his coat of arms. And in the mountains of Cabaret he made men hunt him forsooth with dogs, and with mastiffs, and with greyhounds, even as men hunt a wolf, and he donned the skin of a wolf to make the shepherds and dogs believe him one.[7]

Peire Vidal was badly hurt by the dogs, but he survived to travel through Italy and Hungary. In 1195 he was at the court of the Marquis of Montferrat, and was also patronised by the Marquis d'Este, the Count of Savoy, and the Emperor Frederick II.

Courtly love developed into a code of conduct that it was essential for a true knight to know. In a world dominated by men, the most noble of whom could be boorish and brutal towards women, a knight was the champion of his lady. Women of high birth were political pawns for their fathers or guardians, who married them off in the most advantageous way possible. So a teenage girl could find herself married to a man whom she detested personally. Under the rules of courtly love, a married lady could choose a champion, a knight whose only reason for being was to serve his lady. He could do this by writing poems for her, or by performing noble deeds. Of course this exaggerated courtliness was often a smokescreen for adultery, but it is the framework into which much troubadour poetry fits. Troubadours often addressed their lady as someone of higher status, possibly older, and unattainable. This was very often true. A troubadour could pay an indirect compliment to his patron by praising his patron's wife. This was an accepted thing, as long as the poems did not show too much desire. Bernart de Ventadorn's mistake was that his poetry displayed too much real human feeling towards the Viscountess.

As we have seen, Bernart corrected his mistake, and went to a lady who was a patron in her own right, and powerful enough to protect her own troubadours. Eleanor of Aquitaine was not the only lady who held a court of patronage, however. In southern France there were several centres of culture presided over by women, more so than in other parts of Europe. The reasons for this lie partly in the slightly less subjugated legal status of Provençal women, dating back to Roman times. In 394–5 Theodosius created a code that gave sons and unmarried daughters an equal share in their father's estate. This was brought to southern France in the sixth century by the Visigoths. A code of Justinian, Emperor in the sixth century, also held sway in that part of Europe. It reduced a husband's right to his wife's dowry to *usufructus*; in other words the husband could use the dowry, but not claim ownership of it, or pass it on to his heirs. The rest of Europe favoured the Sallic law, by which a woman could not succeed to an inheritance. By the early tenth century, the counties of Auvergne, Béziers, Carcassonne, Limousin, Montpellier, Nimes, Périgord and Toulouse had all come into the hands of women. By the code of Justinian, Beatrix de Montpellier was able in 1171 to disinherit her son in favour of her daughter and granddaughter. Seen in this light, the ideals of chivalry and courtly love may appear inspired by sycophancy, as an attempt to clothe in attractive garments a means of sucking up to those in power. However, even in Provence, independent women were the exception, and society was controlled mainly by men. The twelfth century, the great century of troubadours, was also the great century of Crusades. Apart from the five great Crusades of 1096, 1146, 1189, 1204, and 1217, there was a constant stream of smaller expeditions eastwards of men bent on recapturing the Holy Land, or at least on having an adventure and cleansing their souls into the bargain. This was a tremendous draw on manpower —approximately half a million men died in the Third Crusade— and often the women were left in control. Almucs de Castelnau was the wife of Guiraut de Simiane, who in 1173 went on a Crusade with his son. In the absence of her husband, Almucs patronised troubadours, and even wrote poetry herself.

One of the most well-known lady troubadours, or *trobairitz*, was Maria de Ventadorn. She was born around 1165, the daughter of Raimon II, Viscount of Turenne, in the Limousin, and Helis de Castelnau. She married Ebles V, Viscount of Ventadorn, and found herself at one of the liveliest courts of patronage in southern France. Ebles II, her husband's ancestor, had been a troubadour, and contemporary of Guilhelm IX of Aquitaine. The court at Ventadorn had patronised Bertran de Born, notably enough for Dante to place him in Hell, and also, of course, the great Bernart. Maria personally patronised many troubadours, including Pons de Capdoill, Gaucelm Faidit, and Gui d'Ussel. One of her existing poems is in the form of a *tenson* between herself and Gui d'Ussel in which she encourages him to sing again despite losing his lady, and in which they discuss aspects of the rules of courtly love:

> Gui d'Ussel, be m pesa de vos,
> car vos etz laissatz de chantar
> e car vos i volgra tornar,
> per que sabetz d'aitals razos,
> vuoill que, m digatz, si deu far egalmen
> dompna per drut, can lo quier francamen,
> cum el per lieis tot cant taing ad amor
> segon los dreitz que tenon l'amador.

> Dompna na Maria, tenssos
> e tot chant cuiva laissar,
> mas aoras non puosc estar
> qu'ieu non chant als vostres somos;
> e respon vos de la dompna breumen
> que per son drut deu far comunalmen
> cum el per lieis, ses garda de ricor:
> qu'en dos amics non deu aver maior.

In English:

> Gui d'Ussel, because of you I'm quite distraught,
> for you've given up your song,
> and since I wish you'd take it up again,
> and since you know about such things,
> I'll ask you this: when a lady
> freely loves a man, should she do
> as much for him as he for her,
> according to the rules of courtly love?

> Lady Maria, *tensons*
> and all manner of song
> I thought I'd given up,
> but when you summon, how can I refuse to sing?
> My reply is that the lady
> ought to do exactly for her lover
> as he does for her, without regard to rank;
> for between two friends neither one should rule.[8]

Several of the existing poems of the trobairitz are in the form of *tensons*, often between a lady and a man, and various aspects and situations of courtly love are discussed. Some nineteenth-century historians liked to maintain that there were actual courts of love, in which any person who broke the rules of courtly love was tried and punished. It is much more likely that the notion stems from these *tensons*. After all, women did not fight, and very rarely governed, so what else was there to occupy the mind?

The poetry of the trobairitz is characteristically open and frank, and less crafted than that of their male counterparts, although so little has survived that it is perhaps unwise to make definitive statements as to why this is. A lady troubadour would certainly not have travelled with her art in the style of the men, and the interchange of styles and ideas would possibly have been decreased as a result, but we know that correspondence between troubadours of both sexes occurred. Moreover, the Countess of Dia wrote poetry that was sophisticated and skilfully made. She was born around 1140, and was from the town now called Die, near Orange. She is close enough in time and place to have been acquainted with the influential troubadour Raimbaut d'Orange, and her technical skill shows that she certainly knew the tradition of which she was a part.

Of the trobairitz whose poems have survived, several held courts of patronage. Tibors is thought to have been the elder sister of Raimbaut d'Orange. She married Bertrand des Baux, and presided over the cultural centre of Les Baux, where the young and orphaned Raimbaut was brought up. It was largely due to his sister's influence that Raimbaut developed into a great patron and also a fine troubadour himself.

It is possible that Raimbaut was a lover, courtly or otherwise, of Azalais de Porcairages, a lady troubadour and patron from a town near Montpellier. Azalais wrote one of the most touching poems that have survived from the twelfth-century troubadours. In 1173 Raimbaut died at the age of twenty-seven, and it has been supposed that Azalais' poem is a complaint on his death:

> Ar em al freg temps vengut
> quel gels el nens e la faingna
> e l aucellet estau mut,
> c'us de chantar nou s'afraingna;
> e son sec li ram pels plais—
> que flors ni foilla noi nais,
> ni rossiguols noi crida,
> que l'am e mai me reissida.
>
> Tant ai lo cors desenbut,
> pe qu' i eu soi a totz estraingna,
> e sai que l'om a perdut
> molt plus test que non gasaingna;
> e s'ieu faill ab motz verais,
> d'Aurenga me moc l'esglais,
> per qu'ien m'estanc esbaida
> e 'n pert solatz en partida

In English:

> Now we are come to the cold time
> when the ice and the snow and the mud
> and the birds' beaks are mute
> for not one inclines to sing;

and the hedge-branches are dry—
no leaf no bud sprouts up,
nor cries the nightingale
whose song awakens me in May.

My heart is so disordered
that I'm rude to everyone;
I know it's easier to lose
than gain; stil, though I be blamed
I'll tell the truth:
my pain comes from Orange.
That's why I stand gaping,
for I've lost the joy of solace.[9]

Much of the poetry of the male troubadours appears stiff, stilted, and artificial compared to this. But much more poetry has survived from the men, and some of them were artists of merit. Dante considered Arnaut Daniel to be worth a mention, and put him in Purgatory in *The Divine Comedy*. He refers to him in these terms:

Fu miglior fabbro del parlar materno[10]

—which Longfellow translates as 'Was of the mother tongue a better smith'. The biography tells us that he visited the court of Richard I, where a jongleur challenged his superiority of writing verse. For a wager, Richard locked them both up for ten days, to see who could come up with the best song. Daniel's inspiration deserted him, but he overheard the jongleur rehearsing his song, and learned it himself. In the contest, Daniel went first, and outfaced the jongleur, but later admitted the truth, and the whole affair was taken as a joke.

The troubadour's poetry tended to glorify love, but it was a sensual, almost pagan love, which was contrary to the teachings of the Church. There were other factors that led to the Albigensian Crusade against Provence. Provence under the Visigoths was the home of a monotheism that denied the unity of Christ and God. Religious beliefs are difficult to stamp out, and Provence readily accepted the Paulician doctrines that were held as heresy by Rome. The Paulician Church was strong in

Constantinople, Thrace, Bulgaria, and Dalmatia, and held the
ancient Manichaeist belief in two unpersonified principles of
good and evil. This was a poor man's religion that rationalised
dogma. In 1167 five Paulician bishops or *prefects* were
consecrated in Toulouse, and Sicard Cellerier became Bishop of
Albi in southern France. Albi became the centre of what became
known as the Albigensian heresy, which was adopted by nobles
all over southern France, including the courts of Aquitaine and
Toulouse. Many found the lack of dogma a means of enjoying
with clearer conscience the sensuality embodied in the
troubadours' songs.

Troubadours found themselves part of a religious controversy.
Peire Cardenal sang about avaricious clergy: 'High felons are
they who sell God, and men undo. They colour their perfidy
under the cloak of honest seeming, they preach unto men, telling
them they are to lead holy lives . . .'[11] Those words were sung
not only in courts, but also in marketplaces. At Toulouse,
Guilhelm Figuiera stirred up anti-Papal feeling: 'Rome—head-
fount of evil and of all our ills. False and perfidious Rome, arch-
cheat and liar.'[12]

Disobedience could not be countenanced, but as usual there
were baser motives than loyalty to the true faith. Provence was
the richest country in Europe. Greedy friars, who were under
Rome's direct jurisdiction, could get no profit out of such an
anti-Papal country. Moreover, Provence was a fief of the crown
of Aragon, and France, champion of the Church, looked on
enviously. In 1209 Pope Innocent III declared a Crusade, and an
army of 500,000 was raised, under Simon de Montfort[13] and the
Papal Legate, Arnold of Citeaux. The Crusade distinguished
itself for butchery. At Béziers the entire population of 60,000
was killed. The Papal Legate, on hearing the objection that many
in the town were loyal, replied: 'Slay them all; the Lord knows
his own.' At the siege of Carcassonne, jongleurs stood on the
walls, singing and playing in defiance. Simon de Montfort
invited Roger de Traucavel, patron of troubadours, to parley,
and then killed him and his fifty companions. In all, three
hundred towns and two hundred castles were completely
destroyed, and all the surrounding countryside was devastated.

Count Raimon VI of Toulouse went to Rome to show penitence, and the Pope called a truce, but Simon de Montfort carried on towards Toulouse regardless. Raimon tried to stop him at the battle of Muret in 1213, but was defeated, and his ally troubadour King Pedro II of Aragon was killed. Simon was killed at Toulouse, but the damage had been done. Southern France lay in ruins, and surviving troubadours lived in exile. Raimon VII of Toulouse reconquered eight years later with Spanish troops, but the wealth and culture of the courts had been wiped out. France gained Provence by the marriage of Louis IX to Raimon Berengar VI's daughter, achieving by diplomacy one of the main objectives of the terrible Crusade.

The heyday of the troubadours was over, but the tradition did not die out. Many of the Provençal troubadours had travelled in Italy, and in the thirteenth century Italian patrons were among the most noted. Count Alberto Malaspina in Lunigiana was famed for his court, and in Sicily Frederick II offered asylum to troubadours from the Papal Inquisition in France. The courtiers in Sicily wrote in Provençal, an indication that the genre was becoming stilted and artificial. The ideals of chivalry were no longer considered realistic, and the rise of a vulgar middle class was altering the nature of literature. By the fourteenth century, Chaucer was treating the attitudes shown in *The Knight's Tale*, a tale of chivalry, as something of a museum piece. However some jongleurs appear to have adapted themselves to changing tastes. Giraut Riquier, a troubadour in exile at the court of Alfonso X of Castile, in 1278 wrote his *Suplicatio qe fes Giraut Riquier al rey de Castela per lo nom del goglars*, a complaint against the coarseness of the tastes of Provençal nobles after the Albigensian Crusade:

> It is unfair that an ignorant man of small learning, who knows a little how to play some instrument and strums it in public places for whatever people will give him, or one who sings low ditties to low people about the streets and taverns, and takes alms without shame from the first comer – that all these should indiscriminately go by the name of joglars[14] . . . For joglaria was invented by wise men, to give joy to good people by their skill in playing on instruments.[15]

Alfonso's reply, also in verse, draws up three distinct classes of entertainer. The first group, the *bufos*, are the men who hang around village greens and marketplaces, combining slender musical talent with more coarse abilities, such as tumbling, juggling and buffoonery. The jongleurs are the second group, musicians and singers fit to appear before noblemen. Finally there are the troubadours, composers of music and poetry. It is probably more accurate to class jongleurs and *bufos* together in the English term 'minstrel', as a class of entertainers from whom the troubadours hired their musicians. Of course, the troubadours would choose the most skilful minstrels, but a minstrel would be more assured of a livelihood if he could vary his talents to suit the tastes of his audiences. Minstrelsy was a tradition widespread and long-lasting, that was utilised by the troubadours in their flourishing, and outlived them.

Notes to Chapter 2

1 Joseph Ritson, *Ancient Songs and Ballads from the Reign of King Henry the Second to the Revolution* (1829), p. 4.
2 'Jongleurs' were musicians, jugglers, tumblers, etc.
3 Geoffrey Chaucer, *Canterbury Tales, The Prologue*, l. 560.
4 Ordericus Vitalis, *Historia ecclesiastica*.
5 H. J. Chaytour, *The Troubadours* (1912), p. 114.
6 Ibid., p. 49.
7 'Peire Vidal', in *The Lives of the Troubadours*, translated by Ida Farnell (1896), p. 86.
8 Meg Bogin, *The Women Troubadours* (1976), p. 98.
9 Ibid., p. 94.
10 Dante, *Purgatorio*, Canto XXVI.
11 Robert S. Briffault, *The Troubadours* (Bloomington, Indiana, 1965), p. 135.
12 Ibid., p. 136.
13 Not the same Simon de Montfort who led the English barons against Henry III in 1264.
14 Or jongleurs.
15 Francis Hueffer, *The Troubadours*, p. 72.

3

MINSTRELS AND PLAYERS

We turn now to England, mainly because minstrelsy was common throughout Europe, and those records most readily available to us are English. The wandering life was common to minstrels, for varying reasons. Those who were lucky enough to be patronised by a noble were only required at his court at certain times. For the rest of the year, they were left to increase their income as best they could by travelling in search of audiences. A great man's minstrel had the protection of his lord, and could expect to be well received at other noble houses. It was considered an honour to be visited by such a man, and to receive him well was courtesy due to his patron.

During Lent, when minstrelsy was not required, a minstrel might visit a school to improve his art. There were schools of minstrelsy at Beauvais, Lyon, and Cambrai. Edward III granted expenses and passports to two bagpipers, Barbor and Morlan, to enable them to visit *Scolas ministrallis in partibus trans mare*.

On the other hand, life was not so easy for those who had no noble protection. The attitude of the Church towards minstrels did not relent, and itinerants could expect to be treated as outlaws. They were constantly on the move, from market to market, and from fair to fair. They could not stay long in one place because simple village folk could not support them well enough, and they could expect rough treatment if they hung around too long. The City and Palatinate of Chester seems to have been a haven for minstrels of the meaner sort. Edward the Confessor favoured Leofric Earl of Chester with a three-day fair at midsummer, during which was an amnesty to all thieves and outlaws. This annual gathering of thieves, pickpockets, minstrels and harlots proved most fortunate during the reign of King John. Randle Blundevil III, Earl of Chester, was in constant conflict with the Welsh, and found himself forced, on one occasion, to retreat to the castle of Rothelent in Flintshire, where he was besieged. He got word to his constable in Chester, Roger Lacy, known as Hell because of his fierce temper, that he was in need of help. It happened to be fair time, and Lacy gathered a host of minstrels, cobblers, pimps and prostitutes, and marched with them towards Rothelent. When the Welsh saw the host coming, they fled. As a reward for his prompt action, Lacy was given power over all the cobblers, minstrels and prostitutes in Chester. His son gave the authority over the minstrels and prostitutes to his steward, Hugh Dutton. From this time developed a tradition by which, each midsummer, Dutton or his descendant would ride to the east gate of Chester, preceded by a minstrel bearing his arms, and there proclaim that all musicians and minstrels in the county-palatine of Chester should approach and play before him. Then after hearing mass Dutton would keep a court, to which all the minstrels had to come and pay their dues. This court had a jury, but it is uncertain to what extent its power reached. We know that the courts were held at least until the end of the fifteenth century because in 1498–9 Henry VII brought a Quo Warranto against Laurence Dutton, demanding why he had received four flagons of wine and a lance, fourpence halfpenny from each minstrel, and fourpence from each harlot. The Duttons' rights were maintained for centuries; legislation against vagrancy in the reign of Elizabeth, and even into the eighteenth century, makes provisos exempting those minstrels in Chester licensed by the Dutton family.

Guilds of minstrels developed regionally, at York, Beverley, and Canterbury. They were for the protection as well as the regulation of their members, but each minstrel had to pay annual dues, and they tended to exclude the lower sorts, widening the rift between 'minstrels of honour' and mere vagrants.

John of Gaunt, Richard II's uncle, seems to have been quite active in personally dealing with the minstrels in his own lands. An entry in his register for 26 November 1373 is a letter to Godefrey Foljaumbe, his seneschal of Newcastle-under-Lyme in Staffordshire. It informs him that from time immemorial minstrels arriving for the fair of St Giles 'pur fair leur ministralcie'[1] have been accustomed to pay fourpence each to William and Margerie de Brompton, and the ancestors of Margerie. The centre of minstrelsy in John of Gaunt's lands was Tutbury in North Staffordshire. Letters patent, dated 22 August 1380, state the charter for minstrels in the honor of Tutbury, encompassing Staffordshire, Derbyshire, Nottinghamshire, Leicestershire, and Warwickshire:

> John, by the grace of God, King of Castile and Leon, duke of Lancaster, to all them who shall see or hear these our letters, greeting. Know ye, we have ordained, constituted, and assigned to our well beloved the King of the Minstrels in our honor of Tutbury, who is, or for the time shall be, to apprehend and arrest all the minstrels in our said honor and franchise, that refuse to doe the service and Minstrelsy as appertain to them to do from ancient times at Tutbury aforesaid, yearly on the day of the Assumption of our Lady (15th August); giving and granting to the said King of the Minstrels for the time being, full power and commandment to make them reasonably to justify and to constrain them to doe their services and Minstrelsies in manner as belongeth to them, and as it hath been there, and of ancient times accustomed . . .[2]

In 1680, Dr Plot witnessed and described the continuing custom of the minstrels' court. The minstrels would assemble at the bailiff's house in Tutbury, and meet the steward and the bailiff. These two gentlemen would accompany the retiring King of the Minstrels in a procession to church, all the other minstrels playing as they went. The King himself had stewards who carried white wands. After the service, the procession went to the castle hall to hold court. The court roll was called, and twenty-four jurors elected, twelve of whom came from Staffordshire. A retiring steward advised the jury: '. . . first commending to their consideration the Original of all Musick, both Wind and String Musick; the antiquity and excellency of both; setting forth the force of it upon the affection by diverse examples etc'.[3] He then warned them to make a careful choice of stewards. Four new stewards were chosen, two from Staffordshire and two from Derbyshire. One of the retiring stewards, alternately from either county, was chosen to be the new King of the Minstrels. After court had been held, they all had a banquet, at which the first toast was to King Blegabres, an imaginary king who was said to have lived before Christ, in the Land of Nowhere.

It was the custom for the Prior of Tutbury to give a bull to the minstrels, 'which bull, as soon as his horns are cut off, his Ears cropt, his Taile cut by the stumple, all his Body smeared over with soap, and his nose blown full of beaten pepper; in short, being made as mad as 'tis possible for him to be',[4] was released on the banks of the River Dove. It was the minstrels' task, immediately after the banquet, to catch the bull before he escaped over the Dove into Derbyshire, and to cut off his hair as a token. The poor bull was then baited in the Bull Ring in Tutbury's High Street. The custom was ended in 1778, because people complained of the violence caused by the bull-running.

In 1387 Richard II granted a passport to John Caumz, *rex ministrellorum nostrorum* (king of our minstrels). This may have been to allow him to visit a school of minstrelsy on the Continent, but it is the title with which we are concerned here. We do not know how official his position was, or how long he held it for, but he is certainly the forerunner of Walter Haliday, who was Edward IV's marshal of minstrels. During the fourteenth century, legislation about itinerant labour had made things difficult for the wandering minstrel. In 1469 Edward IV established a regular guild of minstrels that had authority over all of England, except Chester, and Walter Haliday was its first head, a post he kept for life. His officers could fire any minstrel who practised his trade without paying his dues. In the sixteenth century, the Beverley guild, which was subject to the national guild, restricted membersip to those who were 'mynstrell to some man of honour or worship or waite of some towne corporate or other ancient town, or else of such honestye and conyng as shalbe thought laudable and pleasant to the hearers'.[5]

A statute of the City of Canterbury ordained, in 1526, that all minstrels and waits should be part of a fellowship known as 'the felowshyp of the craft and mystery of mynstrells'.[6] It continues, restricting the practice of minstrelsy:

nor to any p'sonne or p'sonnes, of the seid craft or mystery of mynstrells, to play of any instrument on the Sonday, in tyme of masse or evynsong, in any inne, tavern or any other place, except it be at a weddyng, or a place where he ys hyred, or at the commandement of Master Maier of thys citie, for the tyme beyng, or any other wurshippfull man; and also, except yt be a freman sytting at his owen house to tune hys instrument, or a foren Mynstrell, syttyng at hys ost's, tunyng hys instrument; uppon payne to forfett, for evy tyme doyng the contry, iij s, iiijd (three shillings and fourpence).[7]

The more organised minstrels became, the more difficult circumstances were for the freelancer. The Tudors brought in savage vagrancy laws, which shall be dealt with later, but even without those laws the ordinary itinerant street musician's life was not made any easier by the development of waits. The word comes from the Anglo-Saxon *wacian*, meaning 'watch' or 'guard'. Men were hired by town corporations to pipe the watch in the streets at night. The earliest recorded waits are in York in 1212, and Norwich in 1288. Subsequent cities and towns to keep waits were London, Coventry, Bristol, Shrewsbury, Chester, Beverley, Leicester, Lynn, and Canterbury. They were originally wind instrumentalists, playing hautboys (old-fashioned oboes) and related instruments, but their duties developed from being simply the watch. They wore the town livery, and were available for hire at weddings and other functions, besides being at the disposal of the mayor should he require entertainment. The Norwich waits accompanied Edward IV to France in 1475, and a hundred years later the same band went with Drake on his raid on Lisbon. The existence of a regular town band for hire made it more difficult for other musicians to gain casual employment, especially in smaller towns, and often the law backed this up. In 1582 Leicester town corporation ordered:

noe strangers being mewzicians or Waytes, or other persons whatsoever being either muzicians or players, although they doe or shall dwell within the towne of Leicester and bee not of the companye of the Towne Waytes shall be suffered to playe within the aforesaid towne of Leicester att anye tyme or tymes in the year, att or in a man's housse, dore, wyndowe, or att anye weddings or bryde howses (the time of the general assyses within the towne of Leicester only excepted, and then to playe but only to strangers).[8]

Waits survived to the nineteenth century, by which time their function had declined to no more than the singing of Christmas carols (*see* Plate 2).

Having examined the position of the minstrel in society, we now consider him as a musician and entertainer. A good focal point is the knighting of Edward I's son, on 23 May 1306. The payroll for all the minstrels present at the feast still exists, and it gives us insight into the instruments played. Edward I kept twenty-seven of his own minstrels, but on this occasion there were nearly one hundred present, many of the noble guests bringing their own. By far the most popular instrument was the harp. It was small, portable and simple, but was capable of inspiring brilliant monophonic compositions. Its popularity as national instrument was at its zenith in 1306; with the advent of polyphony it was superseded by more complex instruments. Edward II preferred the *crowd* or *crwth*, an instrument developed from the lyre, played with a bow. It was rectangular, with openings for the hands to reach the strings, and had a bridge and fingerboard. It had six strings, two of which were drones. The crowd lost favour to an instrument that was already becoming popular by 1306, the vielle. This was the ancestor of the violin. In the eleventh century a primitive bow was introduced from the East, and a fretless fingerboard gave the instrument possibilities for an expert to excel. Also present at the feast was the psaltery, an instrument like a harp laid flat over a sound-box. It was more suited to the intimate surroundings of the chamber, and was not the sort of instrument a minstrel might carry around with him.

The feast in 1306 is particularly interesting because in many ways it was a watershed of instrumental development. Besides the harp, still the most popular instrument, though its popularity was to wane soon after, more modern instruments were present, fretted instruments more suitable for the poly-phonic compositions of the fourteenth century. Of the lute, citole and guitar, there was only one each at Prince Edward's

Plate 2 'Town Waits', Leicester, by H. R. Steer

knighting. The lute, smaller and simpler than the Elizabethan lute, was an accompaniment to the voice. It was popular first in Spain, and spread through Europe during the thirteenth century. Janin le Leutour was the only lutenist on royal records between 1285 and 1327, but he was highly thought of, and he received more than almost any other minstrel at the feast. The citole was round or pear-shaped with a flat back and a sweet tone, thought to compliment a woman's voice. The guitar had four strings and a stronger tone than lute or citole. These are the instruments which developed to their height in the Renaissance and, in the guitar's case, beyond; in 1306 they were just beginning to threaten the simple medieval harp.

Wind instruments were also present at the feast, although less in evidence. The trumpet was unfolded until the end of the fourteenth century, and was used more for ceremonial purposes than for entertainment. The fife was played to accompany dancers, jugglers and acrobats, by a musician who would also play the tabor, a two-skinned drum. Acrobats, tumblers and jugglers were not among those entertainers brought by noble guests. Matilda Makejoy, described on the payroll as a *saltatrix*, was a dancer and tumbler who had danced for the King in 1296, and is also on record at court at midsummer 1310. But we have no record of a patron who retained her, and she must have made her day-to-day living away from the court. It is possible that she hired herself out to City guild functions, or travelled around with other acrobats visiting fairs. An engagement at a royal occasion would be a rare piece of good fortune.

Edward I paid some of his minstrels, with the rank of squire, 7½d per day (worth £6.25 in 1978).[9] The others, who were not squires, received 4½d (£3.75). Minstrels were losing their popularity after Edward's death. His grandson, Edward III, kept only thirteen, and none of them received more than 4½d a day. For their part-time work, Edward I's minstrels had an annual income equivalent to £1,500–£2,300. Minstrels of lesser nobles would have had smaller incomes. This basic income was supplemented by the lord's largesse. At Prince Edward's knighting, the King gave out 200 marks,[10] worth nearly £30,000. Of this, Robert Parvus, King of Heralds, received 5 marks

(£750), and William le Sautreour, a psaltery player, and Janin le Leutour each received the equivalent of £500. The largesse was divided unequally between the minstrels, according to their station and the rank of their master. The share given to Matilda Makejoy, and the other independents, would have been small.

Minstrels were sometimes used for political or diplomatic purposes. Because of their profession, they were often allowed freedom of movement during time of war. This is well illustrated by the confession of Robert de Wordreton, at his trial in Paris in 1385. Robert was the valet of an English minstrel called Watier, and his wife Felix. The three of them had set out in September 1384 on a pilgrimage to St James in Galicia, in Spain. The political backcloth is the Hundred Years War. In 1378 Richard II ascended the throne as a boy. Two years later Charles VI came to the throne of France, aged twelve. Charles the Bad, King of Navarre, was trying to enlist English help against the French, to extend his lands in Normandy. When Watier set out, John of Gaunt and Thomas Woodstock were at Calais, while the French regents the Dukes of Berry, Burgundy and Brittany, and the Count of Sancerre were at Boulogne, attempting to negotiate peace. Watier played for the French regents in Boulogne, and returned briefly to London to take money to his children and to buy horses. The three of them then went to Paris, where they stayed for a fortnight and played before the King and other great men. As well as money, they were given robes, a Paternoster of white amber, and a golden ring. They left Paris and travelled south through Orléans, Sully, Bourges, Lyons, Avignon, Béziers and Montpellier, playing at every stop and earning money. Passing through Perpignan and Gonde, they entered Aragon, and played for the King at Parlare. In January 1385 they arrived at Olite in Navarre, where Charles the Bad received them well, being Englishmen. They were there for five days, during which time Charles talked constantly about affairs in France and England. Felix was pregnant, so Watier decided to leave her in Olite and return to Paris to pick up the robes and jewels left there. At this point Robert comes into the story in his own right:

He returned alone to the House of the said King of Navarre, to warm himself and make merry with the royal servants. And he says that while he was quite alone, by the fire of the room, he saw the said King at the door of his chamber beckoning to him and making sign that he wished to speak to him. [11]

The King of Navarre told Robert to buy arsenic sublimate, and to poison the French King and the Dukes of Berry, Burgundy and Bourbon. He also asked him to act as an ambassador to Peter of Navarre, his estranged son. They set off for Paris, Watier continuing to play for noblemen wherever they stopped, and at Bayonne, Robert bought arsenic which he said was to heal a horse's wound. He sewed the poison into his doublet without mentioning it to Watier. When they reached Paris, they decided not to stay, because of the atmosphere created by the death of the Lord of Anjou. He had been killed prosecuting a claim to the Kingdom of Naples. They were ready to leave immediately, but were arrested before they left the Hotel de Mouton, where they were staying. The poison was found, and Robert was tried in front of the Chancellor and Constable of France, the Count of Sancerre, and Jehan de Vienne, Admiral of the Sea. He made a full confession and was executed the next day, 21 March 1385. Watier was vindicated in the confession, and was allowed to go free. We do not know if Watier was the minstrel of some great lord, but he seems to have had a good reputation, judging by the reception he got from kings and dukes. The fact that he had a valet suggests that he was fairly well off for a minstrel.

The wandering minstrel is essentially a medieval figure, but we know that he survived at least into the sixteenth century. Richard Sheale was the Earl of Derby's own minstrel, and he claimed to have written the 'Ballad of Chevy Chase', one of the most popular of medieval English ballads. He used to travel around supplementing his income, and once was robbed of £60, a small fortune in those days. He wrote a ballad about the robbery, in which he tells us that his wife was a seamstress and made money at fairs and markets, at Lichfield and Tamworth, their home town, amongst other places. The song suggests that even the minstrel of an earl is not too well off:

'And without company I ryde along, thus was I folisshe bolde.
I thought beth reason off my harpe no man wolde me
susspecte;
For minstrels offt with mony the be not moche infecte.[12]

The song seems to be part of Sheale's attempt to report his
fortunes, damaged in the robbery, and ends with an appeal to
everyone's sympathy:

Desyryng youe all to bear this tayle in mynde,
That I among your pursis nowe sum frendshipe may fynde.
Everyman a lytell wold satisfye my nede,
To helpe a poor man owt off dett, it ys a gracious dede.[13]

Sheale was one of the last of a dying breed. Later in the same
century, Queen Elizabeth was expected to visit the Earl of
Leicester at Kenilworth, for which great event entertainment
was planned:

az all endeuoour waz too mooue mirth and pastime (az I tolld ye);
eeuen so a ridiculoous deuise of an auncient minstrell and his song
waz prepared to have been profferd.[14]

The minstrel described, with red ribbons and green lace, and the
badge of Islington, is rather a colourful, pantomime version of 'a
squier minstrel of Middilsex, that travaild the cuntree this
soommer seazon into fairz and worshipfull mens hoousez'.[15] He
was regarded as something of an anachronism by the
Elizabethans, and Sheale, in the mid sixteenth century, must
have been something of an unusual figure.

From the fourteenth century to the sixteenth, minstrelsy was
gradually superseded by drama as a popular form of entertainment. English drama has its origins in the miracle and mystery
plays, religious plays performed by members of the medieval
trade guilds. Miracle plays concerned the lives of saints, while the
mysteries told dramatic stories from Scripture. They were
performed on feast days, by amateurs who returned to their own
trade or craft on normal working days. The plays were
performed on huge wooden structures, often with three levels
representing Hell, Earth and Heaven. Each guild produced its

own play, which was part of a cycle. The stages were on wheels, and were dragged from quarter to quarter, so each part of town would receive the different parts of the cycle in succession. The cycles from York, Chester, and Coventry still exist, but in the Middle Ages plays were written and performed all over England. Some of the more adventurous groups of actors travelled with their plays to other towns, and groups of strolling players developed at an amateur level.

The professionals were the liveried servants of great men. Their position was virtually identical to that of the liveried minstrels, except for the fact that as a troupe was required to perform plays a modest gentleman would not be able to afford their upkeep, while he could probably keep a minstrel or two. The King's Players are referred to as early as 1334, when they visited Durham Abbey. In 1390 Richard II and his court were at Skinner's Well, now Clerkenwell in London, watching three days of *interludes*. An interlude was a fairly short play, suitable for a small group of players, and in the subsequent two centuries, until the development of regular theatre, it seems to have been the commonest form of dramatic entertainment. Its position in Elizabethan drama seems to have been similar to that of the Roman mime or Atellan farce. It afforded light relief from the heavier and longer tragedy. It was ideal for a small group of players to take on the road with them, and gave individuals the chance to shine as comic improvisers.

In 1464 Edward IV's Parliament passed the Act of Apparel, controlling the type of clothes different ranks were allowed to wear. Excluded from this were pages, heralds, pursuivants,[16] mayors' sword bearers, messengers, minstrels, and players of interludes. This shows that minstrels and players were considered as the liveried retainers of noblemen, and also that by 1464 players were common enough to be included in the wording of the act. The records of the City of Southampton for 1485–6 demonstrate that players were becoming as essential a part of a lord's retinue as minstrels:

Item payed the 20 Daye of Janyver to my lord of Arundellis mynstrells by Mayster Mayers Comaundment 3/4d . . .

Item payed the 23 daye of the same moneth to my lord of
Arundellis players by Mayster Mayers Comaundment 3/4d . . .[17]

Between 1450 and 1485 Selby Abbey in Yorkshire was visited
by troupes belonging to the Dukes of York and Gloucester, the
Earls of Northumberland and Westmorland, Lord Lovell, Sir
James Tyrrell, Sir Edward Hastings, Sir James Harrington, and
Sir John Conyers. The list reads like the dramatis personae of the
Yorkist faction in *Richard III*. Selby in Yorkshire would have
been worth courting by the Yorkists in the Wars of the Roses,
and it is unlikely that the noblemen's troupes visited the abbey
with the simple motive of giving the monks a good time. Abbots
were rich and powerful men, and the sending and receiving of
players was a diplomatic act that kept relations running
smoothly.

Interludes usually had some underlying political theme, even
when performed by local town or village groups who had
developed from the mystery and miracle tradition. In 1525
Cardinal Wolsey, Henry VIII's chancellor, imprisoned John
Roo, a lawyer, for writing an interlude attacking him. Four
years later the poet John Skelton wrote *Magnyfycence*, an interlude satirising Wolsey, but the chancellor's royal favour was
waning, and the poet got away with it. In 1533 Henry VIII
broke away from the Church of Rome, and this brought new
material for seditious interludes. A priest in Suffolk, John Bale,
was charged with writing miracle plays from the old religion. He
managed to convince his accusers that he wrote Protestant
miracle plays. Pro-Papal plays were performed, though. A
performance in York incited an uprising. In 1539 Spencer, a
priest turned player, was burned at Salisbury for heresy. At the
same time, peasants in Suffolk were using the traditional May
Games of Robin Hood and Maid Marian to spread dissent. In
1533 Henry had forbidden interludes on controversial matters,
but this ruling had been ineffective. In 1542 Sir Richard Morison
suggested to him that the May Game of Robin Hood and Maid
Marian should be replaced by anti-Papal plays 'to set forth and
lively declare to the people's eyes the abomination and
wickedness of the Bishop of Rome, the monks, friars, nuns and

such like, and to declare the obedience due to the King'.[18] To do away with a tradition deeply rooted in folk culture was too much even for the tyrant Henry to attempt, but in 1543 he introduced more stringent censorship. Interludes, books, ballads and rhymes dealing with the interpretation of Scripture were banned. The effect of censorship was to make things more difficult for casual troupes to exist, and led to the gradual establishment of a few trusted groups of professionals, the embryos of the great theatre companies of Elizabeth's reign.

Elizabeth began her reign with an act of censorship. In 1559 religion and the government were banned as subjects for interludes. If players disobeyed, their noble patron was to be held responsible. All plays had to be approved by a mayor, two justices of the peace, or the Lord Lieutenant. This act led to problems. It was a common thing for players to wear the livery of some nobleman or gentleman, and to abscond, using the livery as a passport. In 1616 the Earl of Pembroke issued a warrant for Thomas Swinnerton and Martin Slatier, two members of the Queen's Players, who had left the company and collected a group of vagabonds and idlers together. They had duplicated the Queen's letters patent, and were masquerading as the genuine company.

The usual thing players did when they arrived in a town was to inform the mayor who their patron was:

> In the City of Gloucester, the manner is (as I think it is in other like corporations) that when Players of Enterludes come to towne, they first attend the Mayor, to enforme him what noble-man's servants they are, and so to get licence for their publicke playing; and if the Mayor like the Actors, or would shew respect to their Lord and Master, he appoints them to play their first play before himselfe, and the Aldermen and common counsell of the City; and what is called the Mayor's play, where every one that will comes in without money, the Mayor giving the players a reward as hee thinks fit, to shew respect unto them.[19]

London was as usual one jump ahead of the rest of the country. As early as 1557 enterprising innkeepers at the Saracen's Head, Islington, and the Boar's Head, Aldgate, were hiring out their inn-yards to theatre companies, and charging for entrance to the play. The next step was to install permanent seating. Londoners witnessed the earliest surviving English comedy, Udall's *Ralph Roister-Doister*, and Sackville's early blank-verse tragedy, *Gorboduc*, as well as chronicle plays such as *The Historie of King Leir* and *The Famous Victories of Henry V*, as a prelude to the Golden Age of drama around the turn of the century. Legislation continued to contribute to the development of London as the sophisticated centre of theatre. In 1572 an act was passed to curb the problems of vagrancy, in which players were defined as 'sturdy beggars', and therefore punishable, unless licensed by a nobleman or two justices of the peace. After this date, regional troupes began to die out. The Chelmsford players used to hire out their costumes and props to other towns and villages, but in 1574 they sold off their stock. Braintree, who had once been given a play by Udall, followed suit in 1579, and Bungay in Suffolk folded in 1591. The field was left clear for the professionals. In 1574 James Burbage and four others of Lord Leicester's company were granted a royal licence to act in London and the provinces. The plays had to be vetted by the Master of Revels, and performances were not allowed during the time of divine service or plagues. The London City Council, however, was predominantly Puritan, and asserted its right to censor plays and inns within London. Innkeepers were banned from hosting plays, so in 1576 Burbage built The Theatre, the first permanent theatre, at Shoreditch, outside the City of London. In 1594 his sons were given notice to quit, so they took it down and rebuilt it with the same materials in Southwark. This was the famous Globe, where Shakespeare acted and produced plays, and the design is similar to a large inn-yard.

In 1596 the people of Blackfriars collected a petition for the abolition of the theatre there, which was being extended. A counter-petition was signed by, amongst others, Richard Burbage, William Shakespeare and William Kemp. Kemp was a famous comic actor, who was possibly one of the Earl of Leicester's men in the Low Countries in 1585–6. From there the troupe visited the court of Frederick II in Denmark. By 1590 Kemp had a reputation in London. In *An Almond for a Parrat*, playwright and satirical poet Thomas Nashe makes a dedication to 'that most comicall and conceited Cavaleire Monsieur du Kempe, Jest-monger and Vice-gerent generall to the Ghost of Dicke Tarlton'. Kemp was well known for his jigs, either for writing them or for immortalising them with his own flashes of improvised wit. A jig was a rhyme sung by the clown after a play, that sometimes included dancing to the pipe and tabor. Another playwright, John Marston, included in his play *The Scourge of Villainy* the line

The orbs celestial will dance Kempe's jig.[20]

In 1596 Kemp was with the Lord Chamberlain's Servants, playing at the Globe in the summer and Blackfriars in winter. He took such parts as Dogbery in *Much Ado About Nothing*, Justice Shallow in *Henry IV Part 2*, and the gravedigger in *Hamlet*. In 1599 he danced from London to Norwich dressed as a morris dancer, and published his account of the journey (*see* Figure 2). He was accompanied by Thomas Slye, who played the pipe and tabor, his servant William Bee, and George Sprat, who made sure he danced all the way without cheating. He calls himself 'myselfe, thats I, otherwise called Cavaliero Kemp, head-master of Morrice-dancers, high Head-borough of heighs, and onely tricker of your Trill-lilles and best bel-shangles betwene Sion and mount Surrey'.[21] The whole jaunt lasted four weeks, but much of that was resting, and the actual dancing took nine days. People came out and danced along with him for stretches, and he was even met by Sir Thomas Mildmay, an important man at court. He arrived at Bury St Edmunds just as the Lord Chief Justice arrived at another gate, and seems to have upstaged him:

The wondring and regardles multitude making his honor cleere way, left the streetes where he past to gape at me, the throng of them being so great that poore Will Kemp was seaven times stayed ere hee could recover his Inne.[22]

The dance was performed in Lent, and Kemp had to wait at Bury St Edmunds for six days while snow cleared. The condition of the road must have been terrible, but this clown, who must have been in his late thirties, tells his own story as if it were one big joke. When he got to Norwich the mayor entertained him and gave him £5, quite a gift in those days. He was welcomed by the Norwich waits, given an annuity of forty shillings, and made a freeman of the merchant venturers. His motives for such an eccentric stunt may have been financial. Besides gifts from the City of Norwich, he made money on bets, but had difficulty in collecting his winnings. He would also have made some profit out of the sales of *Kemp's Nine Daie Wonder,* which he says he wrote 'to satisfie his friends the truth against all lying ballad makers'.[23]

Kemps nine daies vvonder.
Performed in a daunce from
London to Norwich.

Containing the pleasure, paines and kinde entertainment
of *William Kemp* betweene *London* and that Citty
in his late Morrice.

Wherein is somewhat set downe worth note; to reprooue
the slaunders spred of him : many things merry,
nothing hurtfull.

Written by himselfe to satisfie his friends.

LONDON
Printed by *E. A.* for *Nicholas Ling,* and are to be
solde at his shop at the west doore of Saint
Paules Church 1600.

Figure 2 Frontispiece to Kemp's original publication

While those with exceptional talents, like Kemp, came to London and became part of the established theatre, troupes continued to travel under the patronage of noblemen, although the spread of Puritan attitudes meant they were received more and more frostily. In 1632 the City of Southampton records:

> March 6th given to a company of Players to send them away 2/6d.[24]

Two years later the tone is more intolerant:

> September 7 Payd unto Prinse Charles Players to rid them out of towne £1.[25]

In 1642 Parliament suspended all plays, and six years later abolished them completely. Players were classed as vagabonds 'notwithstanding any license whatsoever from the King or any person or persons to that purpose'.[26]

Drama was dead for the time being. It was revived with the restoration of Charles II in 1660, but the medieval tradition of liveried troupes of entertainers was over.

Notes to Chapter 3

1 *John of Gaunt's Register*, edited by Sydney Armitage Smith (1911), Vol. 2, p. 98, n. 1105.

2 Sir John Hawkins, *A General History of the Science and Practice of Music* (1875), Book V, Chapter XLII, p. 192.

3 Ibid., p. 193.

4 Ibid., p. 194.

5 E. K. Chambers, *The Medieval Stage* (1903), Vol. II, p. 261.

6 William Welfitt, *Minutes from Ancient Records in Canterbury* (1802), No. XXI, supplement to minutes.

7 Ibid.

8 Jonathan E. O. Wilshere, *Leicester Towne Waytes* (Leicester 1970), p. 4.

9 All these monetary equivalents are for 1978. The rate of inflation at the time of writing makes any attempt to update them pointless.

10 A mark was 13s. 4d., two-thirds of a pound.

11 'The Adventures of an English Minstrel and his Varlet', translated by Bertram Schofield, in *Musical Quarterly*, Vol. 35, No. 3 (1949), p. 361.

12 *Songs and Ballads, with Other Short Poems, Chiefly of the Reign of Philip and Mary*, edited by Thomas Wright (1860), No. XLVI, pp. 156–61.

13 Ibid.
14 In Chambers, *The Medieval Stage*, Vol. II, p. 263.
15 Ibid.
16 'pursuivant': a junior herald or nobleman's attendant.
17 C. E. C. Burch, *Minstrels and Players in Southampton 1428–1635* (Southampton 1969), p. 14.
18 M. C. Bradbrook, *The Rise of the Common Player* (1962), p. 31.
19 In Burch, p. 16.
20 Sir Edmund Kerchever, *The Elizabethan Stage* (1923), Vol. II, p. 325.
21 *Kemp's Nine Daie Wonder*, edited by Alexander Dyce (1840), p. 3.
22 Ibid., p. 11.
23 Ibid. p. 3.
24 In Burch, p. 37.
25 Ibid.
26 Ibid.

4

'FOND BOOKS, BALLADS, RHIMES AND OTHER LEWD TREATISES IN THE ENGLISH TONGUE'

We now consider the position of the minstrel or ballad singer as a political figure, and society's attitude towards him. With the Norman conquest, many *gleemen* found themselves thrust out of their positions by the new overlords. They became part of an undercurrent keeping alive the spirit of English resistance. Heroic songs about Hereward the Wake, who resisted the Normans for some years after Hastings, were sung from village to village by the itinerant musicians. Although they did not present a real threat once William the Conqueror had established himself, a strong sense of separate identity between English serfs and Norman overlords carried on for much longer. The fame of English folk heroes, such as Robin Hood, became an integral part of peasant lore. All the peasants were illiterate, and the only place they would go that was outside their own village would be a market or a fair, where they might hear a ballad about Robin Hood and Maid Marian, sung by a wandering singer. The influence that itinerant musicians had was considerable. William Longchamp, Bishop of Ely and Richard I's chancellor, was an unpopular man, and he thought it worthwhile to hire minstrels to sing his praises in public places all over England.

A nation that the foreign invaders found more difficult to subdue was the Welsh. The Welsh had their own tradition of bards, and their own language and literature. It was closely related to Breton culture, and it is thought that the Welsh bards originated the legends of Arthurian romance, which had found their way into the mainstream of European literature by the fifteenth century. The status of bards was defined by Howel Dha in 920, and by Gruffyd ab Cynan in 1100. The highest were the *pryddyd*, or chair bards, worthy to sing at the prince's chair. Also respected were *teuluwr*, or palace bards, and *arwydd fardd*, or heralds. As might be expected, the official bards looked on the *clerwr*, or wandering bards, with contempt, but it was these wanderers who kept alive the spirit of Welsh disaffection with English rule. In 1284 Edward I attempted to suppress by proclamation 'Wasters, bards, and rhymers and other idlers and vagabonds, who live on the gifts called Cymortha'.[1] This was an explicit attack on the Welsh bards. We can see how unsuccessful it was, or how resilient the *clerwr* were, by Henry IV's legislation of 1402:

> That no wasters and rhymers, minstrels or vagabonds, be maintained in Wales to make kymorthas or quyllages on the common people, who by their divinations, lies, and exhortations are partly cause of the insurrection and rebellion now in Wales.[2]

Welsh rebellion was an issue of nationalism. The English serfs also had their dissident singers, but over the centuries as the aristocracy became more English it became an issue of class more than of nationality. The peasants were continually disaffected,

Figure 3 The hurdy-gurdy was a popular folk instrument in the Middle Ages and has changed little since. The handle turned a wheel that vibrated the strings, rather like a violin bow. One string was a drone but the others were fretted by mechanical keys, and the instrument could be described as a mechanical violin

but in the fourteenth century events accelerated the changing structure of society, causing social upheaval and unrest. In 1348 the Black Death struck England with particular severity and killed a large part of the work force. The immediate result was that labourers found their services at a premium, and could choose, to a certain extent, the master who paid higher wages, despite Edward III's attempt to prevent them from doing so. The feudal system had already been in decay. Serfs had begun to pay their feudal dues in money rather than service. The labour shortage of the fourteenth century meant it was much easier for a serf to abscond for a year and a day, and become a free man. However, the corollary was that the working man's traditional attachment to the land was broken down, and landowners became more exclusively in control of their lands. With the development of the wool trade, it became profitable to turn arable land into pasture, and many serfs were turned off land that their families had farmed for generations. Movements of dissidence began to come into the open. John Wycliffe preached against the wealth and corruption of the clergy, gaining a steadily growing group of followers who called themselves Lollards. William Langland wrote his great poem *Piers Plowman*, a cry of independence for the common man against the dual oppression of feudal and ecclesiastical hierarchies. John Ball travelled around markets and crossroads, and even preached in the fields as serfs worked, spreading the doctrine of equality for all men. His verse sermons started with the famous couplet that in 1381 was on the lips of virtually every serf in the South East:

> When Adam delved and Eve span
> Who was then the gentleman?

In 1380 Richard II's regents attempted to impose a poll tax, to curb vagrancy. The following year Ball was imprisoned for inciting sedition. The peasants revolted, led by Wat Tyler, and freed Ball. The rebels were eventually outfaced by the nobles, and Tyler killed, but that was not the end of unrest. In 1400 Henry IV tried to suppress the Lollards by ordering the burning of all heretics. William Sautrey, a parish priest, was immediately burned. Dating from this time are the songs of Jacke Upland, against the friars of Rome selling absolution, and other abuses in the Church. The language is common English, and Jacke Upland is a figure representative of the common countryman:

> And these men hav all manner power
> of God, as they seyn,
> in heaven an in y earth,
> to sell heaven and hell
> to whom that them liketh . . .[3]

A group of friars collaborated to write replies, calling themselves Daw Topias; the style is more rhetorical and polished:

> Ho shal graunten to myn eye
> a strong streme of teres,
> to wailen and to wepen
> the sorwynge of synne?[4]

In 1450 England was suffering from the weak government of Henry VI. Henry's favourite, the Duke of Suffolk, was an unpopular figure, and he was killed in a rebellion of the men of Kent, led by Jack Cade, an Irish soldier. A ballad rejoicing in his death calls him Jac Napes:

> In the monethe of May, when gresse groweth grene,
> Flagrant in her floures, with swete savour,
> Jac Napes wolde one the see a maryner to ben,
> With his cloge and his cheyn, to seke more tresour.
> Suyche a payn prickkede hym, he asked a confessour.
> Nicholas said, 'I am redi thi confessour to be,'
> He was holden so that he ne passede that hour.
> For Jac Napes soule *Placebo* and *Dirige*.[5]

Throughout the fifteenth century the process of turning arable land into pasture continued, and the problem of vagrancy increased. The Reformation made matters worse. The dissolution of the monasteries in the 1530s took away a source of charity to the needy, while at the same time turning a great many monks out onto the roads with no means of living. There was much Tudor legislation that tried to curb the effects of

vagrancy, without attempting to alter the causes. In 1530 Henry
VIII ruled that beggars who could not work required a licence to
beg. Pardoners, fortune-tellers, fencers, minstrels and players also
had to have a licence, without which they could be whipped on
two consecutive days. Three years later Henry issued a
proclamation to suppress 'fond books, ballads, rhimes and other
lewd treatises in the English tongue'.[6] The specification of the
English tongue suggests that it was still a mark of dissidence.

In 1547 Edward VI's regents brought in a much more severe
law. Any able-bodied man without a job was considered a
vagrant, and could be branded with a 'V', and given two years as
a chained slave, mending roads. If he tried to run away, he was
enslaved for life, and a second escape was punishable with death.
The severity of the law was tempered two years later, but the
attitude of the establishment towards vagrants remained harsh.
The Privy Council sent countless letters to justices of the peace
and sheriffs urging them to uphold the law, and to organise
regular watches to catch vagrants. The frequency of these letters
suggests that enforcement in the provinces was lax, and many
country people were sympathetic to vagrants, risking a heavy
fine for harbouring them, rather than handing them over.

In 1572 Elizabeth legislated to establish a poor relief for those
in genuine need. Minstrels, players, and bearwards were
pronounced 'sturdy beggars' (ie beggars capable of work) unless
they could gain a licence from two justices of the peace.
Provision was made for convicted vagrants to work on stocks of
wool, hemp, and iron. But the causes of vagrancy were not
altered, and in 1588 the numbers on the roads were increased by
soldiers and sailors returning home from the wars. Establishment
figures did not appreciate that social conditions created vagrancy,
seeing wilful idleness as the main cause:

> A company of idle youths, loathing honest labour and dispising
> lawful trades, betake themselves to a vagrant and vicious life, in evey
> corner of Cities and market Townes of the Realme, singing and
> selling of ballads and pamplets full of ribaudrie, and all scurrilous
> vanity, to the prophanation of God's name, and withdrawing
> people from christian exercises, especially at faires, markets, and
> such publike meetings.[7]

Phillip Stubbes thought minstrels, even with a licence, were the devil incarnate:

> I thinke that all good minstrelles, sober and chast musiciens (speking of suche drunken sockets and bawdye parasits as range the cuntreyes, ryming and singing of uncleane, corrupt, and filthie songs in Tavernes, Ale-houses, Innes, and other publique assemblies) may dance the wild Morris thorow a needles eye . . . if you would have your sonne softe, wommannish, uncleane, smoth mouthed, affected to bawdrie, scurrilitie, filthie rimes, and unsemely talking; brifly, if you wold have him, as it weare, transnatured into a woman, or worse, set him to dancing school, and to learn musicke . . .
>
> But some of them will reply, and say, what, Sir. we have lycenses from iustices of peace to pype and use our minstralsie to our best commoditie. Cursed be those licences which lycense any man to get his lyving with the destruction of many thousands.[8]

It is probably true that many vagrants were so because they did not want to work. A subculture developed, which had its own doggerel, and many of the songs are in fact of the low moral standard complained of by Stubbes and many other Puritans:

> Doxy oh, thy Glaziers shine
>   As Glymmar by the Salomon,
> No Gentry Mort hath parts like thine
>   No Cove e're wap'd with such a one.
>
> White thy fambles, red thy gan,
>   And thy quarrons dainty is,
> Couch a hogshead with me than,
>   In the Darkmans clip and kiss.
>
> What though I no Togeman wear,
>   Not Commission, Mish, or slate
> Store of strummel wee'l have here
>   And i'th' Skipper lib in state.[9]

The seventeenth-century translation offered by Head attempts to avoid impropriety, but conveys the general meaning:

My honey chuck, by the Mass I swear
Thine eyes do shine than fire more clear,
No silken Girl hath thighs like thine,
No Doe was ever buck'd like mine.

Thy hand is white and red thy lip,
Thy dainty body I will clip,
Let's down to sleep our selves then lay,
Hug in the dark and kiss and play.

What though I no cloak do wear
And neither Shirt or Sheet do bear,
Yet straw wee'l have enough that's sweet
And tumble when i'th' Barn we meet.

The bad reputation that vagrant ballad singers had in Elizabeth's reign was not totally unjustified but, as is usually the case, there were some more worthy than others. Sir Philip Sydney, courtier, statesman, soldier, and fine poet, was one voice in favour of them:

Certainly I must confess my own barbarousness. I never heard the old song of Percy and Douglas, that I found not my heart moved more than with a trumpet. And yet is it sung but by some blind Crowder, with no rougher voice than rude style.[10]

In London, the sale of printed ballad sheets in the streets by singers became a common thing. The earliest of these ballad sheets still extant is about the death of Thomas Cromwell in 1540, expressing joy at his downfall. During Elizabeth's reign the industry grew, many of the songs being critical of the government. The most famous ballad writer was Thomas Deloney, a weaver, who increased his income by selling novels and ballads in the streets. He wrote a 'Ballad on the Want of Corn', which came to the notice of the Lord Mayor of London, Sir Stephen Slany, because 'it contained in it certain vain and presumptuous matters, bringing in the Queen, speaking with her People Dialogue wise in very fond and undecent sort'.[11] Deloney and his singer, Matthew Nash, were both imprisoned. Deloney wrote to the Lord Mayor justifying his ballad, and seems to have been let go, while for Nash the incident was the start of his good fortune. He was interviewed by Lord Cecil, and not only did he clear himself of any charges, but he also impressed Cecil to such an extent that with his patronage he was able to retire from the uncertain profession of street singing.

In years of high prices, when the weaving trade found itself often idle, Deloney kept himself alive by writing ballads and novels for sale on the streets. His novels include *Iacke of Newberie*, *The Gentle Craft (i)*, *The Gentle Craft (ii)*, and *Thomas of Reading*. In *The Gentle Craft (ii)* he invented the character Anthony-Now-now, a street fiddler, otherwise 'the firkin Fidler of Finchlane'.[12] He gets his name from a song he sang outside the house of a cobbler, which he did for free because the cobbler was out of work and short of money:

> When should a man shew himselfe gentle and kind,
> When should a man comfort the sorrowfull minde?
> O Anthony now, now, now,
> O Anthony now, now, now.[13]

The fictitious Anthony seems to have taken on some kind of representative significance for street musicians. Chettle, another writer, makes Anthony's ghost protest against abuses in the profession, caused by men teaching indecent ballads to young children. He particularly accuses a man called Barnes, who was frequently in Bishop Stortford, in Essex:

The olde fellow their father, soothing his sonnes folly, resting his crabbed limes on a crab-tree staffe, was wont (and I thinke yet he uses) to sever himselfe from the Booth, or rather Brothell of his two sons Ballad shambels: where, the one in a skweaking treble, the other in an ale-blowen base, carrowle out such adultrous ribaudry, as chast eares abhorre to heare, and modestie hath no tongue to utter.

While they are in the ruffe of ribaudrie . . . the olde ale-knight, their dad, breakes out into admiration, and sends stragling customers to admire the roaring of his sonnes: where, that I may showe some abuses, and yet for shame let slip the most odious, they heare no better matter, but the lascivious under songs of Watkins ale, the Carmans whistle, Chopingknives, and frier foxtaile, and that with such odious and detested boldnes, as if there be any one line in those lewd songs than other mor abhominable, that with a double repetion is lowdly belowed . . . The father leapes, the lubers roare, the people runne, the Divell laughs, God lowers, and good men weepe.[14]

Chettle goes on to insinuate that these performances are in collaboration with pickpockets. This certainly had some truth in it. In Ben Jonson's play *Bartholomew Fair* (1614), Nightingale the street musician is seen working with pickpockets as part of a team. Jonson knew London at street level, and would not have invented such a scene.

Some ballad singers became well-known figures. 'Outroaring Dick' Cheetre was from Essex, and was possibly the best known. He regularly frequented Braintree Fair, and could reckon on earning ten shillings in a day, quite a good sum by working men's standards. His rival was Will Wimbars, who supposedly stuck to a select list of favourite songs he knew were successful. The songs were published by various offices situated in the Seven Dials, in London. The most successful publisher was Jemmy Catnach of Monmouth Court. His office flourished throughout the seventeenth century, and well into the eighteenth. He kept a violinist in his offices, and if a writer brought in a ballad he would hear it sung on the spot to a well-known tune. If he liked it he would buy it for two shillings and sixpence. His offices boasted a stock of 4,000 different ballads for sale. They were printed on broadsheets, often with a woodcut illustration. These woodcuts would usually bear no relation whatsoever to the subject of the song, having been bought second hand from sales of printers' stock, and would be just to catch the eye. Apart from political songs, the ballads often told historical tales, such as the assassination of Henri IV of France in 1610, or the Massacre of Amboyna in 1623. They served the purposes of newspapers in keeping the people up to date with the latest news, and reflecting popular feelings. Ballads about oddities, such as a pig-faced lady, and about disasters sold well. Murders were very popular, and the last dying speeches of notorious criminals sold like hot cakes. Publishers like Catnach could have ballads on the streets for sale

Figure 4 The violin often accompanied street ballads

literally hours after the execution, or whatever event, had taken place. There were street singers on every corner singing their ballads and attempting to sell their copies, and the fact that offices such as Catnach's survived so long shows that people must have bought them in thousands.

In 1656 Oliver Cromwell prohibited all fiddlers or minstrels from playing in taverns, and from offering their services in public. However, four years later Charles II was on the throne. All such prohibitions were lifted, the fiddlers were on the streets again, and Catnach's was back in business.

Samuel Pepys made a collection of street ballads dating from the period 1595–1639. Of the 1,671 ballads in his collection, 964 are unique, and they represent a valuable social document of the thoughts, opinions, amusements, and fears of ordinary people in Tudor and Stuart London. The other major collector of ballads was John Bagford (1650–1716), a shoemaker.

The ballad singer survives into the eighteenth century (*see* Figure 4). Sir Richard Steele was amongst the educated bourgeoisie who took notice of them:

> At the corner of Warwick St, as I was listening to a new ballad, a ragged rascal, a beggar who knew me, came up to me, and began to turn the eyes of the good company upon me, by telling me he was extreme poor, and should die in the streets for want of a drink, except I immediately would have the charity to give him sixpence . . .[15]

Other literary figures took a more active part in the scene. Annual festivals were held at St Giles, London, and these were frequented by Steele, Bolingbroke, Gay, and Swift. Swift was an extremely active satirical pamphleteer, and he also wrote ballads to supply the singers. In this way he managed to ensure that his 'Our Johnny is come from the wars', a severe satire directed against the Duke of Marlborough, was sung on every street corner in London. It is said that the Duchess would not forgive him until he wrote *Gulliver's Travels*. Gay also wrote ballads, but he probably did it for the money, being poorer than Swift until his opera was a success. In 1728 he brought out his *Beggar's*

Opera, which was wildly successful. Many of the songs and tunes were taken from street ballads. It was one of those rare occasions when popular and establishment culture meet with harmony. The ballad singers saw it as a moral victory for low life, and viewed Gay with admiration rather than jealousy. A public house where they met once a week to hold a ballad market, exchange songs, and drink and sing together was renamed the Beggar's Opera. Clara, a street singer who had originally sung 'Black-eyed Susan', and one or two other songs from the *Beggar's Opera*, was the object of the attentions of Lord Bolingbroke. Gay was a made man, both financially and socially. It is best to end this chapter on a high note for low life, leaving the fate of later street singers to a later chapter.

Notes to Chapter 4

1 In Chambers, *The Medieval Stage*, p. 54, n. 3.
2 Jean Adrien Antoine Jules Jusserand, *English Wayfaring Life in the Middle Ages* (University Paperbacks 1961), p. 113.
3 *Political Poems and Songs Related to English History Composed During the Period from the Accession of Edward III to that of Richard III*, edited by Thomas Wright, (1859), Vol. 2, 'Jacke Upland', p. 16.
4 Ibid., 'The Reply of Friar Daw Topias', p. 39.
5 Ibid., 'On the Death of the Duke of Suffolk', p. 232.
6 *The Mirror*, 9 July 1825.
7 *The Works of Thomas Deloney*, edited by F. O. Mann (Oxford 1912), Introduction, p. X.
8 *Phillip Stubbes's Anatomy of the Abuses in England in Shakespere's Youth*, edited by F. J. Furnivall (1877–9), Part 1, p. 171.
9 Richard Head, *The Canting Academy* (2nd edition 1674), p. 19.
10 Sir Philip Sidney, *An Apology for Poetry*, edited by Geoffrey Shepherd (Manchester University Press 1973), p. 118.
11 In Mann, Introduction, p. IX.
12 Ibid., *The Gentle Craft (ii)*, Chapter X, p. 204.
13 Ibid., *The Gentle Craft (ii)*, Chapter X, p. 205.
14 Frank Aydelotte, 'Kind-Harts Dreame', in *Elizabethan Rogues and Vagabonds* (Oxford 1913), p. 48.
15 *The Spectator*, No. 454, 11 August 1712.

5

COMEDIANS
AND MOUNTEBANKS

In thirteenth- and fourteenth-century Italy, theatre began to revive from the Dark Ages, and with it blossomed a tradition that was peculiarly Italian, the *commedia dell' arte all 'improviso.* It is generally accepted that the *commedia* was descended from the mime artists forced onto the road when the Roman theatres were closed by the Lombard invaders in AD 568. The Renaissance comedians travelled around in groups, taking stage, scenery and costumes with them, and setting up in marketplaces and squares to play in the open air. Their great talent was comic improvisation and, like the Roman mimes, they used slapstick techniques. Other similarities were the masks worn by comic characters such as Harlequin and Pulcinella, and the phallus worn by Scaramuccia and Pantalone. The pantomime had been the origin of the mask, but it had degenerated from its cultural peak long before the theatres were closed. The phallus had originally been associated with the rites of Bacchus, but had been adopted by the mimes for their own obscene comedies. A shaved scalp had been in vogue amongst the ancient mimes, and this was imitated by the later comedians who used head-bands and false scalps.

One of the best-known characters from the *commedia* is Punch, or Pulcinella. It has been suggested that he is descended from the Roman clown Maccus. Like Punch, Maccus had a big nose and a hunched back. He also had a stage habit of hopping like a chicken, and was sometimes called Pullus Gallinaceus, which may have become corrupted to 'Pulcinella'. There are other theories about the origins of Punch. One is that he takes his name from a thirteenth-century patriot, Pulcinella dalle Carceri. Another theory says he dates from the sixteenth century:

A troupe of itinerant comedians one day came upon a group of peasants gathering grapes in the vicinity of Acerra.[1] Both actors and vintagers had drunk too deeply, and soon the two factions fell to baiting one another. One of the peasants, Puccio d'Aniello by name, a corpulent wag with a long nose and a ready wit, was particularly sharp in the exchange of repartee. At length biting words gave way to blows, and the Thespians were put to rout. But when both parties had finally recovered their tempers and good sense the comedians, remembering Puccio d'Aniello's clever tongue, invited him to join their troupe. He accepted, and straightaway became one of their most popular members. And his costume when on the stage was none other than the same white linen shirt which he had always worn in Acerra.[2]

Another figure to survive from ancient times was the swaggering soldier. In Plautus he was Miles Gloriosus, but by the Renaissance had turned into Capitano Matamoros, or Capitano Spavento della Valle Inferna. He was modelled on the Italian *condottieri*, or mercenaries, but in the sixteenth century became a Spaniard, reflecting the Italian people's hate of their foreign oppressors. He was a boaster, like Shakespeare's Pistol or Falstaff, but was a figure to be made a fool of by the clowns.

Other characters developed over the centuries, different parts of Italy giving different stock types. University town Bologna gave the foolish and pedantic Dottore, while Venice with its merchant adventurers gave the old miser Pantalone. The mountainous region of Bergamo, in the north, was supposedly inhabited by slow-witted rustics, and the buffoons or *zanni*, Arlecchino and Brighella, come from there.

The plays performed by these characters did not have regular scripts. Instead, scenarios were printed and posted in the wings, reminding the actors of the general plot. It was up to the actors to improvise around the plot structure, and much of the humour came from the *lazzi*, or comic business, that accompanied the improvised dialogue. For instance clowns would pretend to catch and eat flies, or to spit cherry pips into the face of another actor while he was speaking, and acrobatics formed a large part of the comic repertoire. Below is part of the scenario for the comedy of *Contratti Rotti*, about a wedding contract:

Act 1

Leghorn

BRIGHELLA	enters, looks about the stage, and, seeing no one, calls.
PANTALOON	frightened, comes on.
BRIGHELLA	wishes to leave his service, etc.
PANTALOON	recommends himself to him.
BRIGHELLA	relents and promises to aid him.
PANTALOON	says (in a stage whisper) that his creditors, especially TRUFFALDINO, insist on being paid; that the extension of credit expires that day, etc.
	At this moment:
TRUFFALDINO	(scene of demanding payment)
BRIGHELLA	finds a way of getting rid of him
PANTALOON and BRIGHELLA	remain.
	At this moment:
TARTAGLIA	comes to the window and listens.
BRIGHELLA	espies him. He and PANTALOON pretend to be very wealthy.
TARTAGLIA	comes down into the street. He goes through the 'business' of begging for alms from PANTALOON. In the end they agree to a marriage between TARTAGLIA's daughter and PANTALOON's son.[3]

The scenario is typically one of rich men being duped into marriage contracts, creditors being avoided, and confidence tricks being pulled. It is up to the actors to make as much as possible out of it, and there was every opportunity for talent to shine. One of the greatest scenario writers was Flaminio Scala. He was an actor who travelled with the famous sixteenth-century company, the Gelosi, with the stage name Flavio. He left fifty scenarios, of which forty were comedies, one a tragedy, and nine eleborate fantasies called *opera regia*. Usually scenarios were the property of the troupe of their writer, but Scala's collection was published in 1611.

The most prolific writer in the history of the Italian comedy was Carlo Goldoni, a Venetian. He really belongs to the eighteenth century, and was responsible for introducing written plots instead of scenarios. Always a prolific writer, he once produced sixteen plays in one season. When he was in his eighties, although still producing plays, he found time to write his memoirs as well. His recollections of running away from school in Rimini with a troupe of players travelling by ship convey something of the picturesque side of an itinerant actor's life:

> . . . this troupe in the ensemble aboard ship was a droll spectacle to behold. There were a dozen people—as many actors and actresses—a prompter, a stage-carpenter, a property-man, eight men-servants, four maids, nurses, children of all ages, dogs, cats, monkeys, parrots, birds, pigeons, a lamb—it was a Noah's Ark.[4]

Harlequin.   Zany Cornetto.

Non,non,n'eftime pas en couranr en barbet, En clabaut ou maftin,me rauir Frácifquine, Ie veux eftre pendu maintenant au gibet, Si plus vifte que toyfur les mains ne chemine.

Ie fay l'arbre fourchu, portant les pieds en l'ær, Pour (difpoft) triompher en fi haulte conquefte Ettoy plus l'ourd qu'vn Ours, ne fçaurois reculler, Ny aller en auant, tanttu és groffe befte.

Dy ce que tu voudras, ie feray des premiers Au côbat amoureux, que fur tout ie pour chaffe, Il n'eft chaffe œ tout tèps q de bôs vieux limiers, Qui fçauér des cônils le terroir & la trace   iiij.

Figure 5 Harlequin and Zany cornetto

It sounds romantic, but life on the road had its dangers and difficulties. Apart from the dangers such as bad weather, poor roads, or bandits, it was as likely as not that the authorities of whatever town was visited would prove hostile, from jealousy, superstition, or religious zeal. Beltrame da Milano, otherwise Niccolo Barbieri, describes what happened in 1596 when he and a clown called Montferrin arrived in a town in Savoy and asked for permission to erect their platform:

> The governor . . . not knowing what course to follow betook himself to his spiritual adviser, who refused the permission instanter, saying that on no account should magicians be allowed in the country. Montferrin was stupefied, and protested that since he did not know how to read it was hardly possible for him to make magic. The superior bade him be silent. 'I know what you rogues do,' said he; 'I have seen mountebanks in Italy pass a ball from one hand to the other, and put a little piece of lead in one eye and make it come out of the other. I have seen them swallow fire and blow forth flames and sparks; thrust a knife through the arm and not suffer from the wound; and all this they do by enchantment and other works of the devil.' Whereupon the superior sent Montferrin away, nor would he listen to his remonstrances, but threatened him with prison. . .[5]

This kind of opposition was more from ignorance than anything else. Some people thought *histriones* meant *stregoni*, or sorcerers. The Church was not unilaterally opposed to the *commedia*. Adriano Valerini, who was with the Gelosi, was forbidden to perform by the governor of Milan, but the archbishop, Charles Borromeo, later made a saint, read the scenarios and approved them, and the shows went on.

By the sixteenth century certain troupes had acquired a skill and a reputation that took them to the courts of kings and nobles all over Europe. The troupe of Alberto Ganassa was one. In 1568 they were in Mantua, where at the command of the Duke they combined for one performance with the troupe of Flaminio Scala. In 1570 they were part of the wedding festivities of Lucrezia d'Este at Ferrara, and the following year they were in Paris for the entry of Charles IX and his young bride. The French *parlement* sent them away, accusing them of charging too high a fee, but they were back in 1572 for the marriage of Marguerite de Valois and Henri of Navarre. From there they went to Madrid, where that most proper Christian Renaissance king Philip II entertained them at the Escorial, and vice versa, for five years. Ganassa himself was the first recorded Arlecchino, or Harlequin, and if he did not invent the part, at least he was responsible for immortalising it.

Not all of Ganassa's troupe went to Madrid. Some of them stayed in Paris and formed the Gelosi. The name comes from their motto: 'Virtu, fama, ed onor ne ser' gelosi', or 'They were jealous of attaining virtue, fame, and honour.' They were in Venice for the carnival in 1574, and then at Milan at the request of Don John of Austria. In 1576, the company that went to Austria to visit the Emperor consisted of the following:

Innamorato (or Lover), then	
Capitano Spavento	FRANCESCO ANDREINI
Dottor Graziano	LUCIO BURCHIELLA
Pantalone	GIULIO PASQUATI, of Padua
Zanne (Arlecchino)	SIMONE, of Bologna
Franca-trippa	GABRIELO PANZANINI
Flavio	FLAMINIO SCALA
Innamorato: Orazio	ORAZIO MOBILI, of Padua
Aurelio	ADRIANO VALERINI, of Verona
Zanobia da Piombino (old man)	GIROLAMO SALIMBONI, of Florence
Prima Donna	LIDIA DE BAGNACAVALLO
Seconda Donna	PRUDENZA, of Verona

In 1577 they were captured by the Huguenots and held to ransom. They were eventually freed, and reached Paris at Henri III's invitation. They were a great success performing at the Hôtel de Bourbon, but despite letters patent from the King, Parlement sent them away. The following year Francesco Andreini succeeded Flaminio Scala as director, and married Isabella. They spent the next few years touring Italy, and in 1586 Prince Vicenza of Mantua honoured the Andreinis by accepting their daughter as a godchild. In 1588 the troupe went once more to Paris, and more opposition from the French parlement, which banned all comedians and acrobats. Henri III's power was decidedly shaky, and in that year the War of the Three Henris broke out, leaving two of the Henris, the Duke of Guise and the last Valois King of France, dead. In such a political climate the Gelosi thought it unwise to stay, and they returned to Italy.

Once peace returned to France, so did the Gelosi, at the request of Henri IV for the reception of his bride Marie de Medici. In 1604 they were in Paris when Isabella Andreini died of a miscarriage. After this, the troupe returned to Florence and disbanded. At that time the company still included Francesco Andreini, Giulio Pasquati, and Simone of Bologna, after twenty-eight years of wandering around Europe.

The son of Francesco and Isabella, Giovanni-Battista Andreini, formed a new company, the Comici Fedeli. Several of the actors from the Gelosi joined the troupe, and they inherited the scenarios of the old company. These were added to by the writings of Giovanni-Battista, which were mostly obscene. In 1613 he received a letter from Marie de Medici, by then the Queen Mother:

> For your private ear, Harlequin . . . You may be assured of the King's good graces. My son and I remember what you desire for the baptism of the child your wife is to bear, and shall have ready the gold chain which has been promised you. I wish to give it to you with my own hands without trusting it to any of my subordinates, for I know how ill disposed you are toward any intermediaries. The sooner you set forth, the greater will be your welcome. Come, then, with all speed . . .[6]

Of course the Fedeli accepted an invitation couched in such intimate terms from a queen. They played at court, and at the Hôtel de Bourgogne, and were as successful as usual.

The great troupes of the Renaissance, the Gelosi, the Fedeli, the comedians of Harlequin and Scaramouche, were welcomed at courts all over Europe, and honoured by princes, queens, and dukes. But despite royal or noble patronage, they were liable to some of the same risks that their less successful brethren lived with. Comedians who had to be content with an open-air stage, or perhaps a barn in a country village, travelled the roads unprotected from persecution that often stemmed from religious bigotry. They were vagabonds, and could be treated with contempt or worse by whomever they met. Those who had the patronage of a great man could still suffer similar persecution in an age when life on the roads was virtually lawless. And favour extended by a patron could be withdrawn at whim.

In 1658 the stage at the Hôtel de Petit Bourbon was shared by two companies. The regular theatre-going days, Sunday, Tuesday and Friday, witnessed the performances of the Italian comedians of Tiberio Fiorelli, known as Scaramuccia, or Scaramouche. On the remaining days of the week, the troupe of Molière took the stage. Two of the greatest figures of seventeenth-century comedy, each in his own way, gracing the capital of the young Louis XIV makes a brilliant focal point. But the stories behind the figures show how chequered could be the lives of even the most lauded artists. Molière earned his exalted place in the history of French literature through a hard apprenticeship in which the Italian *commedia* was not uninvolved.

Molière was born Jean-Baptiste Poquelin in Paris in January 1622. His father was *valet de chambre tapissier du roi*, or upholsterer by royal appointment to Louis XIII. They were middle class and well off, and in 1637 the succession of his father's office was settled on young Jean-Baptiste. But there were other influences at work. The Poquelin house was near the Pont-Neuf, on which comedians and quacks used to set up their stages and entertain the public. The influence of the Italians had spread to the native comedians, and the French characters Gros-Guillaume and Guillot-Gorjut displayed some of the characteristics of Harlequin and Dottore. From the open-air planks of the Pont-Neuf these and other French comedians rose to the success and fame of the Hôtel de Bourgogne. Jean-Baptiste was taken to this theatre by his grandfather on several occasions, despite his father's protest that it would turn him into a comedian. In 1632 his mother died, leaving an emotional void that was partly filled by the old man, who owned two booths at the fair of St Germain des Près, and it was this influence that ultimately proved stronger than the attractions of becoming the king's upholsterer.

In 1642 Jean-Baptiste may have gone to Narbonne in the train of Louis XIII, officiating for his father, who was too busy. Whether or not it was on this trip that he met Madeleine Béjart does not really matter. The fact remains that the Béjart family played a large part in the rest of his life. She was four years older than him, and had already been on the stage for seven years when he fell in love with her. She, her elder brother Joseph, and her younger sister and brother, Geneviève and Louis, were strolling players, who were already not unknown in Paris. Molière's detractors have tried to maintain that Madeleine Béjart was a loose-living woman of low character. In fact, she had been the mistress of Esprit de Remond de Mormoiron, Baron of Modene, and bore his child, but she had been seduced by his false promises, and she was always loyal to Molière. It may have been the death of Monsieur Béjart senior, leaving the family only debts, that persuaded them to join Molière's first romantic scheme, the *Théâtre Illustre*.

Cardinal Richelieu had been fond of the theatre, and he had persuaded Louis XIII to proclaim that no aspersion should attach to the profession of player. But actors were still classed as vagabonds, social and religious outcasts. Jean-Baptiste Poquelin's idea was to create a company of respectable amateurs who would play for free in fashionable circles, thereby raising the status of theatre. In January 1643, on attaining his majority, he received the inheritance left him by his mother, but it was not enough to finance his dreams, and in June of that year the company signed a contract, making them professional actors. It was at this point that he assumed the name Molière. All the actors were from the bourgeoisie. Monsieur Béjart had been a minor official at court. The names on the contract include Nicolas Bonnenfant, a lawyer's clerk, André Maréschal, a parliamentary advocate, George Pinel, a writing-master, and Catherine Desurlis, the daughter of a record clerk to the Privy Council. Between them they hired a vacant tennis court to be transformed into a theatre, and they were even confident enough to have the road widened and paved in anticipation of carriages. While this building was taking place, they made their professional début at Rouen fair, with four fiddlers to attract custom.

The company opened in Paris in January 1644, and was a complete flop. They hired a dancer to dance interludes in an attempt to liven up the audience, but it was still no good. Nobody came to see them perform their tragedies. Molière convinced himself that their failure was due to the situation of the theatre, in an unfashionable part of town, so the following year they moved to another, more expensive venue. He could not believe that it was the acting and the plays that were keeping the audiences away. French drama at the time was a very stiff affair. It held very strictly to Aristotle's rules of the three unities of time, space, and action. Because of this, long narrative monologues were necessary to fill in parts of the story that could not be enacted on stage. Plays were written in Alexandrine verse, lines of twelve syllables, with an obligatory pause at the sixth, in couplets of alternating masculine and feminine rhymes (a masculine rhyme ends in a mute *e*, while a feminine ends in an accented *é*). Prose was only allowable in farces that were full of low buffoonery, which without the Italian genius for improvisation could be a very mediocre spectacle. Molière was never a good tragic actor, and he found himself in prison for debt in 1645. He managed to get security for his release from the man who had paved the street outside his theatre, and set out on the road with the Béjart family and those remaining who had not been disillusioned. The *Théâtre Illustre* was a failure, and now they were vagabonds, strolling players. For Moliére's father, who had given him the best education and brought him up to continue the family's honourable position, this must have been a bitter fact to accept, but it was he who eventually paid off the large debts run up by his son.

They set off with all the ladies, props, and belongings in an open cart, with the men walking, and headed towards Bordeaux, the capital of Guyenne. Somewhere on their travels they met a company led by Charles Dufresne, an experienced comic actor, and the two companies joined forces under his leadership. The governor of Guyenne was the Duc d'Epernon, and he became their patron. This was fortune of a kind, but they still spent most of their time wandering around country towns and villages, playing in barns, sleeping in straw, and running the gauntlet of bandits and police alike. In 1648 the outbreak of the Fronde made life even more dangerous. The King was only ten years old, and some nobles tried to seize the opportunity of furthering their own lawless ends. The countryside swarmed with bands of marauding soldiers, who often were not sure whose authority they recognised. The Duc d'Epernon was at war with Bordeaux, and his players found that Guyenne was no longer a hospitable place for them. It is said that Limoges was so hostile that twenty years later Molière wrote the comedy *Monsieur de Pourceaugnac* in revenge.

The troupe turned eastwards towards Lyons. Lyons was at the crossroads of Italian, German and Provençal merchants, and was a lively and important city. It was also a provincial artistic centre that was almost as prestigious as Paris. Here in 1653 Molière presented his first comedy, *L'Etourdi; ou les Contretemps* (*The Blunderer; or the Mishaps*). He borrowed the plot from Niccolo Barbieri's farce *L'Inavvertito*, which itself claimed descent from Plautus. Although Molière's version was presented in five acts, and in Alexandrine verse, it was still a farce in the Italian style in terms of the situations the characters found themselves in. It was a great success. Three others of Molière's early comedies survive, showing a strong Italian influence. They are *La Jalousie du Barbouille* (*The Jealousy of Smutty Face*), *Le Médecin Volant* (*The Flying Physician*), which is an adaptation of Scaramouche's *Il Medico Volante*, and *Le Dépit Amoureux* (*The Love Tiff*).

While they were enjoying their first success, they were summoned by Armand de Bourbon, Prince de Conti, of royal blood. This young prince had been a rebel in the Fronde, but in 1653 he made peace with Cardinal Mazarin, the King's protector. Mazarin offered Conti a complete amnesty and the governorship of Languedoc if he married his niece, Anna Martinozzi. Conti was at Château La Grange des Près in Languedoc, preparing himself for this, when his mistress Madame de Calvimont expressed a whim for the players. Molière was sent for, but in the meantime, a troupe under a comedian by the name of Cormier was at nearby Pézenas, and Madame de Calvimont decided she wanted the more immediate gratification of her desires. When Molière's troupe finally arrived, they were told to go away and refused payment for their journey. The Abbé Daniel de Cosnac, who had been instrumental in inviting the comedians, was on the point of paying them himself, but instead his secretary persuaded him to command a performance in his own name at La Grange des Près. It was a great success, and the audience was delighted, with one exception. Madame de Calvimont refused to laugh, and so Conti still turned his back on the comedians. But after a second performance, the applause was so great that Conti had to send Cormier away (and Madame de Calvimont followed soon afterwards). The troupe of Dufresne and Molière became the comedians of the Prince de Conti. In 1654, after marrying Mazarin's niece, Conti became governor of Languedoc, and he called a meeting of *Les Etats* at Montpellier over the winter of 1654–5. This body had in the past been an influential power in government, but under the despotism of Louis XIV it became simply a gathering of all the richest and most fashionable families in Languedoc. Molière was required to entertain this brilliant assembly, and he and his comedians at last began to realise financial as well as artistic success. During this period the comedians were paid so well that Madeleine Béjart was able to lend the province of Languedoc 10,000 livres.

The Prince de Conti had led a dissipated life of debauchery and political intrigue. He was a man of capricious moods, and in 1653 he turned his favour on Molière's troupe. But as Madame de Calvimont had found out, this was no guarantee of security. In 1656 Conti, at the age of twenty-eight, suddenly became a religious fanatic, turning to the puritanical Jansenist doctrines. Comedy, dancing and gaming were banished from his court, and Molière and his actors found themselves on the road again, without employment or protection. Languedoc became a hostile place. Any police they met were Conti's, and they treated comedians little better than outlaws. The troupe turned north again, and eventually in 1658 came to Rouen, where they stayed until an opening could be found at Paris. It is not certain how they first attracted the notice of the court, but it has been suggested that Corneille, who lived at Rouen, had some hand in it. He was in his fifties, and already a respected man of letters, and he is said to have fallen for the charms of one of Molière's

actresses, the Italian Marquise Thérèse du Parc (Marquise was her
Christian name, not her title).

In October 1658 the troupe were summoned to an audience
with Monsieur, the King's eighteen-year-old brother, who was
looking for a company to rival Louis' troupe of the Hôtel de
Bourgogne. The company presented Corneille's tragedy
Nicomedes to the court, who were not much impressed. Molière
himself took the stage and apologetically flattered the King,
begging permission to continue with a farce. They presented the
playwright's own *Le Docteur Amoureux* (*The Amorous Doctor*),
and Louis XIV himself laughed. The company became The
Troupe of Monsieur, Only Brother of the King, and were
immediately granted a pension by the delighted young prince,
which, typically, was never paid. By Louis' permission, they
moved into the Hôtel du Petit Bourbon, sharing the days of
performance with Scaramouche's Italian company, who were
already established.

The story of the production and success of Molière's great and
famous plays does not directly concern us. From 1658 until his
death in 1673 he stayed in Paris, enjoying royal favour, wealth,
and public acclaim. Although remembered by posterity as a
playwright, he was also an actor, and continued against the
advice of his friends, until the end. Even on the day of his death
he acted, ironically the lead role, in the début of his last work, *Le
Malade Imaginaire* (*The Hypochondriac*). What does concern us
however is the social stigma that he never managed to shake off,
despite the favour of the most absolute monarch the world has
seen. Many considered him to be an upstart courtier, and the
cutting satire of his plays earned him enemies. In 1659 *Les
Précieuses Ridicules*, a play whose title is virtually untranslatable,
set all Paris laughing at the *précieuses*, groups of women whose
attempts to establish literary coteries had become ridiculous by
the extremes to which they took adherence to fatuous and
extravagant codes of behaviour. Even the most simple salutation
had to be clothed in classical allusions or gratuitous
ornamentation. Revenge was swift. Monsieur Ratabon,
superintendent of the King's buildings, began to demolish the
Hôtel de Petit Bourbon without notifying the actors, claiming

the site was needed for planned extensions to the Louvre. Louis reacted by giving Molière the theatre in the royal palace, which had fallen into disuse.

Molière had many detractors. In 1662 he married Armande Béjart, who, at twenty, could have been the sister or the daughter of Madeleine Béjart. Molière's enemies claimed that he had married his own daughter, or at least the daughter of his lover. This would have been a crime against the Church, and in those days could have led to severe penalties. Louis refused to listen to those who came to him accusing Molière of an immoral marriage, and showed his contempt for them by becoming the godfather of the first child of the union, Louis.

Molière's father was still a *valet de chambre*, but he was getting old, so Molière took over the duties, which included the honour of making the King's bed every so often. When Molière's turn came, the other valets refused to have anything to do with a player, a mere vagabond. They refused to eat at the same table as him. This came to the ears of the monarch, who invited Molière to share his breakfast. While they were eating, the King summoned the other valets to watch.

Although Louis XIV made considerable gestures of personal favour towards him, even at his death Molière experienced the prejudice that all actors suffered. While he lay dying, his family sent out for priests. Two refused to come to the aid of an actor, and the third came only after much persuasion, and by the time he came it was too late to hear a confession. Two nuns, who were living on Molière's hospitality, stated that he had made a good Christian end. But Armande his widow had a great deal of difficulty in gaining permission for a Christian burial. The barest minimum of ritual was allowed at the funeral, which took place at night, with only one priest. In the eyes of the Church, Molière lived and died a vagabond.

Less is known about Tiberio Fiorelli, Molière's colleague at the Hôtel de Petit Bourbon, who, although considerably older, outlived him. He was born in Italy, around 1604. He was the son of a cavalry captain, and was brought up constantly on the move, and often in trouble with the law. He was tall, agile and graceful, and could sing and play the lute with accomplishment.

He joined a small troupe of comedians at Fano, and was an instant success with Scaramuccia, a character of his own invention. Scaramuccia, or Scaramouche as he is universally called, inherited the swagger of the Capitano, something he must have learned from his father's associates. He was not specifically a soldier, though, and wore black robes. He started off with the mask, but at some point in his career discarded it, and powdered his face white. He became one of the greatest exponents and developers of the art of grimace, an art descended from the ancient mimes. He was first noticed by the Duke of Mantua, who gave him an introduction to noble patronage. Once he had broken into the European 'circuit', he continued to rise. In 1639 he went to Paris at the head of a troupe, at the invitation of Cardinal Mazarin. They stayed there for nine years, until the outbreak of the Fronde in 1648, when they returned to Italy. When peace returned, so did the Italians. The Parisians were by now coming to expect the presence of the Italian comedians in their midst. Scaramouche was universally admired as one of the greatest comic actors of his day. During the period of his coexistence with Molière, the Frenchman used to send young actors to watch him, as the model of a natural mode of acting. Molière considered Fiorelli's influence on French theatre to be a powerful one in ridding French actors of their traditional 'demoniacal tone'; French actors had been known to self-induce apoplexy and literally kill themselves from over-acting.[7] The Italians were more relaxed, with the appearance of a casualness that was in fact the result of a great talent for comic improvisation. A French *fariné* or white-faced comedian called Jodelet, who learned the art of grimace from Fiorelli, joined Molière's troupe, but unfortunately died soon afterwards.

Fiorelli was also the recipient of Louis XIV's favour. In 1664 he was granted a pension of 15,000 livres. It is uncertain when he died, but in 1688, when he was in his eighties, he married and produced a child, and he was still acting at the time.

Not even the protection of Louis XIV could be relied on for ever. In 1683 Louis fell under the attractions of his last mistress, Madame de Maintenon. His life up until then had been one of licentiousness, but at the age of forty-five he started to reflect upon his soul, and the pious Madame de Maintenon presented an alternative existence. Under her influence, the tone of the court veered towards prudery. The Italian comedians were ordered to curtail the lewdness of their jokes and gestures. In 1697 a novel, *La Fausse Prude*, was published in Holland, transparently about Madame de Maintenon, and the Italians immediately responded with a play of the same title, in Italian *La Finta Matrigna*. They were immediately banned from the theatres, and also from within thirty miles of Paris.

While the theatres were closed, the Italians played at the fairs, but even here they met with opposition. The Comédie Française were granted a monopoly on the acting of plays. The Italians showed great resilience and ingenuity in getting round the prohibitions. Sometimes a scene would be acted with only one actor taking all the parts. Another dodge was for all the actors to mime as if they were writing their lines on paper, and one actor spoke all the lines, pretending to read what was written. They were forbidden to speak at all, but that did not defeat them. In 1713 *Arlequin Roi de Serendib* was acted at the St Germain fair in silence, the dialogue being written out on scrolls which were unrolled in sequence, and those members of the audience who could read read them out for the benefit of the others. The *commedia* in France hung on until 1716, when Louis XV's regent invited them back to Paris. By this time, the Italian tradition was being taken over by Frenchmen, and when in 1780 the Théâtre des Italiens was established in Paris, it had no Italians at all.

Related to the Italian comedian is the mountebank, or quack doctor, by virtue of the fact that he also made a living out of his talents for improvisation. Although the name is of Italian derivation, *montare* to ascend, and *banco* a bench, the type is more universal. There have always been characters ready to live on their wits and on the credulity of others. Ancient Egypt had its mountebanks, as did classical Greece and Rome. The age-old method of the mountebank has been to gain his audience's confidence, either by conjuring tricks or simply by using long words in a convincing manner. Mankind's superstition has meant that arcane magical powers have been linked with the arts of healing; quack doctors, having once established a superiority over their audience, found it easy to prey on the latent hypochondria that is still lurking in all of us. One typically disarming method, that of denouncing and denying the very trade being plied, is noticed by Rutebeuf, a thirteenth-century French writer, in his *Diz de l'Erberie*:

> Good people, I am not one of those poor preachers, nor one of those poor herbalists who stand in front of churches with their miserable ill-sown cloak, who carry boxes and sachels and spread out a carpet. Know that I am not one of these; but I belong to a lady whose name is Madam Trote de Salerno, who makes a kerchief of her ears, and whose eyebrows hang down as silver chains behind her shoulders: know that she is the wisest lady that is in all the four parts of the world. My lady sends us into different lands and countries, into Apulia, Calabria, Burgundy, into the forest of Ardennes to kill wild beasts in order to extract good ointments from them, and give medicines to those who are ill in body . . . And because she made me swear by the saints when I parted from her, I will teach you the proper cure for worms if you will listen . . .[8]

The ignorant crowd, charmed by the mention of distant lands and mysterious ladies, fall prey to the mountebank's gullery. The people in power, of course, were always hostile to quacks, not only because they fooled innocent people, but also from their fear of the possibility that they might really have unusual powers. In 1352 Jean le Bon of France issued a decree against mountebanks, accusing them of being 'ignorant of men's temperament, of the time and mode of administering, of the virtues of medicines, above all, of laxative ones in which lies danger of death'.[9]

But mountebanks were no better or no worse than other doctors in the Middle Ages. John of Gaddesden was Edward II's personal doctor, and he tried to cure him from smallpox by wrapping him in red cloth. Gaddesden cannot have known that red light does in fact heal smallpox scars, and medicine was very much a matter of trial and error. In his day the approved cure for gallstones, an ailment that requires surgery, was an ointment made from beetles and grasshoppers.

The mountebank survived for various reasons. One was his

accessibility. He would set up a small stage at fairs, markets or street corners, and anybody could listen to his speech. Even if the man in the street had no money for the cheap medicines on sale, at least he felt that he had in a small way partaken of the mountebank's knowledge. Another reason for the mountebank's popularity was the entertainment he gave. He would often bring music, juggling, conjuring tricks, or even tight-rope walking, and would have the assistance of his *zanies* or clowns. The name 'zanies' comes from the *zanni*, the clowns of the *commedia dell 'arte*. The whole performance could last an hour or two, and many people who felt no need for medicine would watch for the fun of it.

Sometimes the showmanship took over completely, and the mountebank was simply a conjuror or fortune-teller without attempting to foist cures on the public. Henry VIII's statute against vagrants in 1530 included professors of 'physiognomy, palmistry, or other crafty sciences'.[10] And yet Henry's own juggler, Mr Brandon, who was received with honour wherever he travelled, is said to have dabbled in what would have been considered sorcery. He is said to have drawn a dove on the wall of a house on which a pigeon was sitting. After he had stabbed the picture several times, the pigeon, which had been surreptitiously poisoned beforehand, fell dead as if by magic. Brandon was ordered never to do anything of the kind again, but he got off lightly by being in the King's favour. Reginald Scot, relating the story half a century later, complains:

> If this or the like feate should be done by an old woman, everie bodie would crie out for fier and faggot to burne the witch.[11]

Scot was deeply concerned about the persecution of old women accused of being witches by superstitious people. In 1584 he wrote *The Discoverie of Witchcraft*, in which he attempted to dispel superstition by giving scientific explanations for seemingly supernatural phenomena. He devoted a considerable section to the tricks of jugglers and conjurors, exposing many of their best secrets:

The true art therefore of juggling consisteth in legierdemaine to wit, the nimble conveiance of the hand, which is especiallie performed three waies. The first and principall consisteth in hiding and conveing of balles, the second in the alteration of monie, the third in the shuffeling of the cards.[12]

Many of the tricks seem to involve the appearance of physical injury, either to the magician himself, or to some animal or bird. Scot describes how to stick a knife through an arm, or to cut a nose in half, and even how to stick a nail into a chicken's head without killing it. 'The decollation of John Baptist' seems to have been popular at fairs (*see* Figure 6).

To cut off ones head, and to laie it in a platter, which the jugglers call the decollation of John Baptist.

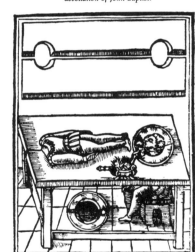

The forme
of ye planks,
&c.

The order
of the acti-
on, as it is
to be shewed.

What order is to be observed for the practising heereof with great admiration, read page 290.

Figure 6 'The decollation of John Baptist'

Another gory trick was to stab oneself in the stomach. To do this a false belly was required, painted as realistically as possible, behind which was a bladder of calf's or sheep's blood, and a protective plate. Scot reminds the novice that the act is no good unless he dies convincingly, and relates how one juggler died all too convincingly:

. . . not long since a juggler caused himself to be killed at a taverne in cheapside, from whence he presentlie went into Powles church-yard and died. Which misfortune fell upon him through his owne Follie, as being then drunken, and having forgotten his plate, which he should have had for his defense.[13]

Although quacks and conjurors were common throughout Europe, a Renaissance Englishman would refer to a 'Venetian mountebank' without a thought of the man's nationality, in the same way that we might use the term 'Roman Catholic' about an Irishman. Thomas Coryat, an English traveller and eccentric, visited Venice in 1608, and described what he saw in the Piazza San Marco, the main square. A lesser type of mountebank, standing on the ground rather than a stage, he calls *ciaratano*, or *ciarlatan*, which he derives from the Greek word to draw a crowd, and from which we get the word 'charlatan'. Those grand enough to have a stage were attended by masked comedians and musicians, who performed an overture while the trunk was unlocked and its magical contents displayed:

. . . after the musicke hath ceased, he maketh an oration to the audience of halfe an houre long, or almost an houre. Where in he doth most hyperbolically extoll the vertue of his drugs and confections . . . Truely I often wondered at many of these naturall Orators. For they would tell their tales with such admirable volubility and plausible grace, even extempore, and seasoned with that singular variety of elegant jests and witty conceits, that they did often strike great admiration into strangers that never heard them before; and by how much the more eloquent these Naturalists are, by so much the greater audience they draw unto them, and the more ware they sell . . . The head Mountebanke at every time that he delivereth out any thing, maketh an extemporall speech, which he doth eftsoones intermingle with such savory jests (but spiced now and then with singular scurrility) that they minister passing mirth and laughter to the whole company, which perhaps may consist of a thousand people that flocke together about one of their stages.[14]

Probably the best example of a Renaissance mountebank's patter is in Ben Jonson's *Volpone*, in which the hero impersonates Scoto of Mantua, supposedly a notorious mountebank. Jonson will have taken his speech from observations made in the streets of London, although the play is set in Venice. The play was written in 1605, before Coryat ever sailed, which proves that Jonson did not choose Venice solely because of what he may have read in one travel book.

Figure 7 Comedians and charlatans in the Piazza San Marco

Volpone displays the classic method, starting by denouncing his competitors as mere imitators and impostors. He also of course denies that his purpose is financial, claiming he has little or nothing to sell. This little or nothing is then described, the most outrageous claims being made for its efficacy. Ben Jonson's combination of rhetoric and quasi-scientific terms was a typical example of the mountebank's method of gaining an audience's confidence:

To fortify the most indigest and crude stomach, ay, were it of one that through extreme weakness vomited blood, applying only a warm napkin to the place, after the unction and fricace; for the vertigine in the head, putting but a drop into your nostrils, likewise behind the ears; a most sovereign and approved remedy: the *mal-caduco*, cramps, convulsions, paralyses, epilepsies, *tremor cordia*, retired nerves, ill vapours of the spleen, stoppings of the liver, the stone, the strangury, *hernia ventosa, iliaca passio*; stops a *dysenteria* immediately; easeth the torsion of the small guts; and cures *melancholia hypocondriaca*, being taken and applied according to my printed receipt.

Pointing to his bill and his glass

For, this is the physician, this the medicine; this counsels, this cures; this gives the direction, this works the effect; and, in sum, both together may be termed an abstract of the theoric and practic in the Aesculapian art. 'Twill cost you eight crowns . . .[15]

Of course, eight crowns is soon reduced to sixpence, purely from the mountebank's philanthropy. Volpone is also accompanied by his zany, who sings songs in favour of the medicine. Jonson has reproduced as complete a picture of the Renaissance mountebank as can be found.

The words 'charlatan' and even 'mountebank' have now become terms of abuse, implying some sort of impostor. But not every mountebank was completely ignorant of medicine. Some merely enjoyed displaying their eloquence and learning in public, and it is possible that the meaning of 'impostor' comes as much from the impersonators of genuinely learned men, as Volpone was impersonating Scoto of Mantua, as from the extravagant claims of the mountebank for his phoney panacea. The Italian nature tends towards the extrovert, and it is not surprising that one of the most renowned mountebanks of the eighteenth century was from that nation. Bonafede Vitali, from Parma, was an ex-Jesuit of good family who studied medicine, and attained the professorial chair at the University of Palermo. But ordinary success was not enough, and he felt the urge to show off his talents as an orator and extempore disputer. He travelled under the name of the Anonymous, and drew crowds wherever he went to speak. Goldoni saw him in Milan in 1734 or 1735:

When at Milan, the Anonymous had the satisfaction of seeing the place where he exhibited filled with crowds of people, on foot and in carriages; but as the learned were far from being the best purchasers, he was obliged to furnish his scaffold with objects calculated to attract and entertain the ignorant multitude, and the new Hippocrates vended his drugs and displayed his rhetoric, surrounded by the four masks of the Italian comedy.[16]

Vitali's comedians were kept at his own expense, and performed whole comedies, as well as helping with the collection. Goldoni made his acquaintance and, although an unknown at the time, was able to assist him. Goldoni had come to know Count Prata, the director of the Milan opera, who was at the time in need of a company, and through his influence he secured the engagement of Vitali's troupe.

Vitali later went to Venice with his comedians, but it was as a doctor that he was famous. The city of Verona sent for him there, to cure an epidemic which had broken out. Having accomplished this he was honoured with the title of first physician of Verona, but did not live long enough to enjoy or benefit from it.

Sometimes, rather than set up in the streets, a quack doctor would have handbills printed and handed out, advertising his presence at some tavern. It was common for him to claim to be just returned from his travels, which lent him an exotic quality that would catch the crowd's attention. In 1712 Steele used the arrival of such a doctor in London as an opportunity to denounce the methods of confidence tricksters:

But the art of managing mankind, is only to make them stare a little to keep up their astonishment, to let nothing be familiar to them, but ever to have something in your sleeve, in which they must think you are deeper than they are.[17]

The doctor in question claims to be able to cure, amongst other things, sea voyages and campaigns, and uses as his testimonial some people who have been lame for thirty years. Phoneys would use the slenderest pretexts to establish their superiority in their professed field:

There is a doctor, in *Mouse-Alley* near *Wapping*, who sets up for curing cataracts upon the credit of having, as his bill sets forth, lost an eye in the emperor's service. His patients come in upon this, and he shews his muster-roll, which confirms that he was in his imperial majesty's troops; and he puts out their eyes with great success.[18]

The progess of medical science was bad for the mountebank's trade, but he survived into the nineteenth century. William Hone witnessed a group of mountebanks who set up on a green in North London in 1826. The party consisted of a clown, a tumbler, and a lady:

The tumbler then reposed by putting a loose coat over his party-coloured habit, and playing a pandean pipe while 'Mr Merriman'[19] sat on a piece of carpet spread on the ground, and tossed four gilt balls in the air at the same time, to the variations of the music. A drum was beat by a woman aged about forty, with a tiara on her head, who afterwards left the beating art and mounting the slack-wire, which was supported by three sticks, coned at each end to a triangle; she danced and vaulted *a la Gouffe.*[20]

Instead of remedies for corns, toothache, or witchcraft, the mountebanks sold lottery tickets for prizes such as teapots and printed calico. There were however still a few street doctors, or *crocuses*, even as late as 1877, when free hospitals and health clubs meant that even the working class could have access to medical treatment. One crocus was particularly sceptical about the skills of genuine doctors:

I expect the dead in this country could tell us summat about poisoning by Act of Parliament . . . I would as soon swallow a brass knocker as some of your drugs . . . Herbs are the thing, they were intended for man and they grow at his feet, for meat and medicine.[21]

Having made this claim to be a genuine herbalist, the crocus then admits that sarsaparilla, sold as a blood purifier, is simply made from sassafras, burnt sugar, water, and pineapple or pear juice. It is essential to wear the right clothes to sell a product. Dressed as a sailor, he can sell any scented root as the Indian root that destroys vermin. Some of the products are genuine, such as cough sweets and ointment, and he ultimately admits that 'a good honest "racket" pays best in the end, people buy and come again'.[22]

The claims of the street doctor got less extravagant as science made inroads into superstition, and the figure who in the seventeenth century might claim to cure all diseases with his own special panacea cuts rather a sorry figure two hundred years later, reduced to selling ointments and throat pills (*see* Figure 8).

Figure 8 Doctor Bokanky, the street herbalist

Notes to Chapter 5

1 In southern Italy.
2 Abbé Galiani, in Pierre Louis Duchartre, *The Italian Comedy*, translated by Randolph T. Weaver (1929), p. 217.
3 Ibid., p. 51
4 *Memoirs of Carlo Goldoni*, translated by John Black (1926), p. 16.
5 In Duchartre, p. 77.
6 Ibid., p. 94
7 Ibid., p. 23.
8 In Jusserand, p. 95.
9 Ibid., p. 96.
10 C. J. Ribton-Turner, *A History of Vagrants and Vagrancy* (1887), p. 74.
11 Reginald Scot, *The Discoverie of Witchcraft* (Centaur Press 1964).
12 Ibid., Chapter XXII, p. 269.
13 Ibid., Chapter XXXIV, p. 20.
14 Thomas Coryat, *Coryat's Crudities* (1611), (Glasgow 1905 edition), Vol. 1, p. 411.
15 Ben Jonson, *Volpone* (1605), Act 2, Scene 1.
16 In Goldoni, p. 127.
17 *The Spectator*, Vol. 6, No. 444, 30 July 1712.
18 Ibid.
19 'Mr Merriman': a generic name for a clown.
20 William Hone, *The Everyday Book* (1831), Vol. II, Column 1292.
21 J. Thomson and Adolphe Smith, *Street Life in London* (1877), p. 19.
22 Ibid., p. 20.

6

FAIRS AND SHOWMEN

The sober merchant and down-at-heel clown may not have had much in common, but they both saw fairs as a means of attaining a common object—money. Their relationship was symbiotic. The gay atmosphere generated by the entertainers attracted more people to the fairs, many of which had been created to facilitate free trade. A large gathering of people with money to spend, combined with the suspension of ordinary taxes, tariffs and regulations, created an environment that was good for business, whether the trade was measurable in yards, pounds, dozens, or less tangibly in laughter.

The earliest fairs of the Christian era developed from gatherings of pilgrims at shrines, abbeys, and cathedrals, on the feast day of the enshrined saint. Many shrines were in open country, and in any case the gathering of a large number of extra people put a strain on whatever facilities existed. The pilgrims needed feeding and accommodating, so merchants readily provided what was required, pitching tents and stalls. The holy men were not slow to capitalise on the situation either, and the imposition of tolls meant a considerable extra income to the Church. Fairs were often held in the churchyard itself. Edward II put an end to this practice in England in 1319–20, but fairs continued to be held in precincts. Anyone who entered was obliged to swear not to lie, cheat, or steal until he left the fair again.

Fairs created the opportunity for increasing the exchange of goods internationally. For example, an English merchant exporting to France would normally have to pay customs tariffs and other taxes that would absorb almost half the value of his goods. But he was exempt if he was travelling to, say, the St Denis fair, held near Paris on 10 December annually. He was also free from arrest while in transit, except for offences committed in the fair. These privileges were forfeit if he should sell any goods out of the fair, or if he left before the end. If he traded after the end of the fair he could be fined double the value of the goods sold.

For the itinerant entertainer, fairs were a golden opportunity to make extra money. The best musicians, jugglers, clowns, and magicians would all converge in a concentration of talent that brought parties of nobles with the sole purpose of seeking pleasure. In Languedoc the nobles went to Beaucaire, in Normandy to Guibray, and in Germany to Frankfort and Leipzig, hoping to find entertainment of a kind better than they got at home. In England the main attraction of this sort was Bartholomew Fair, which will be mentioned later.

One of Europe's greatest fairs in the Middle Ages was Stourbridge Fair, near Cambridge. King John granted the fair to a nearby hospital of lepers. It was held in open countryside on St Bartholomew's Day, and if the corn was not harvested by 24 August the builders were free to erect their booths on top of it. Similarly if the booths were not taken down by Michaelmas noon the ploughmen were free to plough on regardless. The booths were built in streets with names such as Garlic Row, Booksellers' Row, Cook Row, etc. East Anglia was a wealthy area in the Middle Ages, due largely to the wool trade, and vast amounts of cloth, butter, and cheese changed hands. In the Reformation, Henry VIII gave the fair to the City of Cambridge. Parliament banned the acting of plays within ten miles of Cambridge, but a Norwich company obtained special permission to perform at the fair. In 1613 it was reported that at least sixty private coaches came from London, bringing the idle rich to see the amusements of the fair. But the descriptive records pale in comparison to those dealing with London's own beloved, notorious Bartholomew Fair.

Rahere was Henry I's minstrel. About 1102 he went on a pilgrimage to the Holy Land, and was supposedly visited by St Bartholomew in a dream. When he returned to England, following the saint's instructions he founded the priory and hospital of St Bartholomew, becoming its first prior. The site was on the northern extremity of the old City of London, adjacent to West Smithfield, or *Smooth-field*, which was then an open space. West Smithfield was used as a recreation ground by sporting medieval Londoners, and was also the site of a horse-market, occasional jousting, and a gallows.

Rahere secured the grant of a three-day cloth fair from Henry II, as a source of income to the priory. It seems that the showman in him survived his ordination, as he is accused of staging miracles to attract people to the fair. Several supposedly sick people were miraculously healed by the intercession of St Bartholomew. The antiphoner, a large and valuable book, disappeared from the priory, and was discovered by Rahere in a house in the Jewish quarter, the devious prior claiming he had had a vision directing him to it. Rahere was eventually denounced as an impostor by his own monks, but this did not hinder the development of the fair. It was proclaimed annually on St Bartholomew's Eve (23 August) by the mayor and aldermen of London. The following day they would dine in state, and ride to Smithfield to watch wrestling competitions. On the last day of the fair, archery contests would be staged to entertain the dignitaries.

Bartholomew Fair was governed by a Court of Piepowder. This was common to all fairs. Because many merchants, and indeed entertainers, were a long way from home, a machinery of on-the-spot justice was required. The court had jurisdiction over offences committed within the time limits of the fair, and inside the toll gates; once the fair was over, outstanding cases could not be prosecuted. The name is possibly derived from the French, *pied poudre,* referring to the dusty feet of the merchants. Another possible source of the name is *pied puldreaux*, the old French word for itinerant pedlars.

By the end of the sixteenth century, the major commerce of Bartholomew Fair was in pleasure. It had grown so large that it extended across Smithfield and into the surrounding streets. In 1614 James I ordered Smithfield to be paved, as the decline of jousting meant that soft ground was no longer needed. The same year saw the production of Ben Jonson's play, *Bartholomew Fair*, which was performed at the fair with great success. In the play, all the inhabitants of the fair are out to cheat the gullible pleasure-seeker. This is probably quite an accurate picture, but is not peculiar to seventeenth-century London. The professions of pickpocket, pimp, or card-sharp are age-old, and could be found at any fair in any age. However, the late sixteenth and early seventeenth centuries, as we have already noticed, produced many Puritans who were outspoken against the weaknesses of the flesh. An anonymous tract of 1641 unintentionally gives rather a colourful picture of the fair:

> Here, a knave in a foole's coate, with a trumpet sounding, or on a drumme beating, invites you to see his puppets: there, a rogue like a wild woodman, or in an antick shape like an incubus, desires your company to view his motion: on the other side, Hocus Pocus, with three yards of tape, or ribbin, in's hand, shewing his art of legerdemaine, to the admiration of a company of cockoloaches. Amongst these, you shall see a gray Goose cap, (as wise as the rest), with a what do you lacke in his mouth, stand in his boothe, shaking a rattle, or scraping on a fiddle, with which children are so taken, that they presentlie cry out for these fopperies: and all these together make such a distracted noise, that you would thinck Babell were not comparable to it.[1]

Puppets seem to have been a regular feature. Ben Jonson includes a puppet show in his play, and refers to it as if it is part of an old tradition. Although Jonson's puppets are decidedly secular, their manipulator mentions other titles of shows, such as *Jerusalem, Nineveh*, and *Sodom and Gomorrah*, all with a religious theme. Before the Reformation, priests used to exhibit puppet shows as a means of educating while entertaining. In Witney, Oxfordshire, for example, there was an annual presentation of *The Resurrection*. Bartholomew Fair was controlled by the priory of St Bartholomew until the Reformation threw it into the hands of Sir Richard Rich, and it is quite possible that some of the monks forced onto the streets by the dissolution of the monasteries found an alternative livelihood in their puppets. At any rate, the tradition of religious subjects mixed with more light-hearted material was one reason why the Bartholomew puppets escaped the prohibitions of the Commonwealth years.

In 1642 Parliament closed the theatres, and its veto included plays at the fairs. However, the mob had to be humoured to a certain extent, and to ban the fair completely would have been to court trouble. This snippet of doggerel from a collection called *Pills to Purge Melancholy*, published in 1655, describes the amusements tolerated during the interregnum:

> In fifty-five may I never thrive,
>   If I tell you anymore than is true,
> To London che came, hearing of the fame
>   Of a fair they call Bartholomew.
>
> In houses of boards, men walk upon cords,
>   As easy as squirrels crack filberds;
> But the cut-purses they do bite, and rob away;
>   But those we suppose to be ill-birds.
>
> For a penny you may zee a fine puppet-play,
>   And for twopence a rare piece of art;
> And a penny a can, I dare swear to a man
>   May put zix of 'em into a quart.[2]

Punch first came to England in 1666 as Punchinello, an immigrant from the Italian *commedia*. A showman named Powel exhibited puppets under the Little Piazza in Covent Garden, and was so successful with his Punch dancing a minuet with a well-trained pig, that the sexton of the nearby St Paul's church complained that congregations were diminishing and that people were taking the church bells as a signal to come to the show. Powel exhibited shows such as *Whittington and his Cat, Dr Faustus*, and *Friar Bacon*, as well as religious plays, but it was the Italian Punch that won him the greatest popularity. He did not confine his activities to Covent Garden, but was among the attractions at Bartholomew Fair. He was still exhibiting in 1711, when Steele saw him, and by this time he had competitors. A newspaper of Queen Anne's reign advertised:

At Crawley's booth, over against the Crown Tavern, in Smithfield, during the time of *Bartholomew Fair*, will be presented a little opera called *The Old Creation of the World*, yet newly revived; with the addition of *Noah's Flood* . . . besides several figures dancing jigs, sarabands, and country dances, to the admiration of the spectators; with the merry conceits of *Squire Punch*, and *Sir John Spendall*.[3]

Punch is just a small part of the bill here, but his popularity grew immensely. His superiority was challenged during the early nineteenth century by the *fantoccini*, or marionette puppets, which will be described later, but his popularity with children has survived to this day.

Another favourite attraction of Bartholomew Fair was rope-dancing. During the suppression of the theatres, a comedian, Robert Cox, wrote farces which he performed on the tight-rope at fairs, evading the law by appearing as a rope-dancer rather than an actor. With the Restoration in 1660, plays were revived, and Bartholomew Fair was extended to six weeks. Rope-dancing however did not suffer from the revived competition of the theatrical booths. In 1668 the fair was visited by Samuel Pepys:

> There did see a ridiculous obscene little stage-play called 'Merry Andrew', a foolish thing, but seen by everybody; and so to Jacob Hall's dancing of the ropes, a thing worth seeing and mightily followed.[4]

A few days later, Pepys saw him again at Southwark Fair:

> I saw such action as I never saw before, and mightily worth seeing; and here took acquaintance with a fellow that carried me to a tavern whither come the music of this booth, and by and by Jacob Hall himself, with whom I had a mind to speak, to hear whether he had ever any mischief by falls in his time. He told me, Yes, many, but never to the breaking of a limb.[5]

Hall attempted to erect a booth at Charing Cross, but was arrested for it. He was reputedly the lover of Lady Castlemaine, which honour he shared with Charles II, and through her influence he was able to succeed with the Charing Cross venture. He also tried to set up his show in Lincoln's Inn Fields, but the inhabitants petitioned against the idea, and prevented it. In 1683 Hall was hired to dance at a pageant in Cheapside, and Dr Wild immortalised the event in *Rome Rhymed to Death*:

When Jacob Hall on his high rope shews tricks,
The dragon flatters; the Lord Mayor's horse kicks;
The Cheapside crowds, and pageants scarcely know
Which most t'admire, Hall, hobbyhorse, or Bow.[6]

Charles II is well known for his love of pleasure, and during his reign the fair enjoyed royal patronage and protection. Charles liked fairs, and extended Bartholomew Fair to a period of six weeks, as well as instigating another fair in spring, May Fair. However his successors were a little more strait-laced, and the fair comes under fire again towards the end of the seventeenth century. One of the causes for complaint was the mob, known in this instance as Lady Holland's Mob. The trouble dated from 1656 when John Dethick, Lord Mayor of London, had attempted to ban the fair, claiming that it was unofficially proclaimed twelve hours early and that unlawful trading went on during those twelve hours. It had long been the custom for the tailors of London to assemble in the Hand and Shears, a public house in Cloth Fair, by Smithfield, on the night before the Lord Mayor's proclamation. There they would elect a chairman, and at midnight they would all come out of the public house into the street. The chairman would make a speech and declare Bartholomew Fair open, at which all the tailors would snap their shears together and go back into the Hand and Shears. A large crowd would assemble to see the proclamation, and they tended to get excited. In 1656, when the tailors proclaimed the fair, rioting broke out in defiance of Dethick. During the prohibition of the theatres, secret performances took place at Holland House, home of Henry Rich, proprietor of Bartholomew Fair, and the mob took the name of Holland as a mark of defiance against the government. Unfortunately, the rioting became a regular feature, but it was always worst when the mob felt that their traditional right to enjoy themselves was being curtailed in any way. This happened frequently under regimes less broad minded than Charles II's. In 1694 the fair was reduced to the original three days, and three years later the Lord Mayor's proclamation banned 'obscene, lascivious, and scandalous plays, comedies, and farces, unlawful games and interludes, drunkenness, etc'.[7]

Plays were again banned in 1700 and 1702. What made things extremely difficult for the managers of theatrical booths was the fact that these prohibitions were imposed by the Lord Mayor in his speech of proclamation, by which time booths had already been erected, handbills printed, and scenery and costumes made. To run a booth at Bartholomew fair was a commercial gamble that could pay high dividends or be a dead loss.

Already by the turn of the century, some people were calling for the end of the fair, despite the fact that it was still a thriving cloth fair and as a cattle market was at its commercial height. One of these moralists wrote anonymously to *The Observator* in August 1703:

> Does this market of hardness tend to anything else but the ruin of the bodies, souls, and estates of the young men and women of the city of London, who here meet with all the temptations to destruction? The lotteries, to ruin their estates, the drolls, comedies, interludes, and farces, to poison their minds, etc. and in the cloisters what strange medley of lewdness has that place not long since afforded.[8] Lords and ladies, aldermen and their wives, 'squires and fiddlers, citizens and rope-dancers, jack-puddings and lawyers, mistresses and maids, masters and 'prentices. This is not an ark, like Noah's which received the clean and unclean; only the unclean beasts enter this ark, and such as have the devil's livery on their backs.[9]

The fair had too much life in it, and too much popular and powerful support, to be seriously worried by these voices which were as yet in a minority.

The picture of Bartholomew Fair (*see* Figure 9) is taken from the decoration of a fan, dated about 1721. Another part of the same decoration shows a gentleman dressed fashionably, wearing a star and sash. This is thought to be Walpole, Britain's first Prime Minister, and shows that at this period, despite what the detractors might say, it was not shameful for men of high reputation to be seen frequenting the fair. We notice that the unknown artist has not failed to include a pickpocket at work. He also includes Fawkes' booth, one of the best known of the early eighteenth century. Fawkes was a famous conjuror, and is

Figure 9 Part of Bartholomew Fair, 1721

said to have been worth £10,000, a large fortune, when he died
in 1731. He is supposed to have acquired his fortune simply by
being the best conjuror in the country. In the year of his death he
entertained the Algerian ambassadors, and it is said that he
conjured up an apple tree that bore ripe fruit in less than a
minute. We leave this open to the reader's credulity. The report
says that the audience were able to eat the fruit. True or false, the
story gives some indication of Fawkes' reputation as a magician,
and if one does not believe in magic, one must at least credit him
with being a top-class showman.

Outside Lee and Harper's booth, on a platform, we can see
amongst other characters a clown and a harlequin. It was the job
of these comedians to attract custom, and very often an
illustrious career started on the boards outside. We borrow a
report from May Fair, the fair that gave its name to an exclusive
part of London:

> A 'Mountebanke's Stage' was erected opposite the Three Jolly
> Butchers' public house[on the east side of the market area, now
> the King's Arms]. Here Woodward, the inimitable comedian and
> harlequin, made his first appearance as merry-andrew; from these
> humble boards he soon after found his way to Covent-garden
> theatre.[10]

The name *merry-andrew* is said to derive from Andrew Boorde,
a famous English mountebank of the early sixteenth century.
Boorde was an extremely learned doctor by the standards of his
time, and published, amongst other more light-hearted works, a
Breviary of Health. He was also an incorrigible traveller and by all
reports an extremely amusing man. The term *merry-andrew* was
virtually synonymous with 'zany', and came to mean any clown
placed on a stage to act the fool. The merry-andrew would not
necessarily be part of a mountebank's show. He might be simply
a freelance comedian, and many theatrical booths hired them to
perform on a platform outside to attract the crowds. Because of
the din of the fair, it was a position for which mime was ideally
suited and some merry-andrews were great artists. But not all, as
the *London Spy* of 1699 tells us. A merry-andrew demonstrated:

a singular Instance of his Cleanliness, by blowing his Nose upon the People, who were mightily pleas'd, and Laugh'd heartily at the jest . . . [it was] a Tale of a Tub, illustrated with abundance of ugly Faces and mimical Actions; for in that lay the chief of the Comedy . . .[11]

If we could accept the merry-andrew's invitation to step inside the booth, we would quite possibly be surprised at the standard of drama presented. During fair time the London theatres were closed, and all the professional actors walked the temporary boards at Smithfield. There was also a fair amount of talent behind the scenes. Henry Fielding, author of *Tom Jones* and one of England's greatest novelists, spent nine years with theatrical booths. After an education at Eton and Leyden University, he was pushed into the world by his father, with an allowance of £200 a year, to make a career for himself. He declared that his choice lay between being a hack writer and a hackney coachman. In 1728 he partnered a booth-owner, Reynolds, at Southwark Fair, with a production of Gay's *Beggar's Opera*, performed by the entire Haymarket company. The following year, Colley wrote the *Beggar's Wedding*, an imitation of Gay's famous and successful work. This played in Dublin, and subsequently at the Haymarket Theatre. It then went to the Drury Lane Theatre, with Fielding as Justice Quorum, and the same company performed it at Fielding's booth in the George Inn Yard, Smithfield, during Bartholomew Fair. The Haymarket company thought this was unfair, and ran a rival production of the same piece at another booth in the fair, but Fielding bribed their leading man, Hulett, to join the Drury Lane company. In 1732 *The Earl of Essex* was a great success at the fair. It was Fielding's adaptation of *The Forced Physician*, by Molière. Prince George, later George II, and his wife watched the play, and stayed for a second showing. The following season saw Fielding's *A Cure for Covetousness*, an adaptation of Molière's *The Cheats of Scapin*, in which the maid, Loveit, was played by an unknown actress making her début. This unknown was Mrs Pritchard, who later became one of the eighteenth century's most celebrated actresses.

Besides adapting and producing established works, Fielding also wrote his own original pieces, some of which he sold to other companies. A newspaper of 1734 advertises:

> At Fawkes and Pinchbeck's Great Theatrical Booth, the end of Hosier Lane, the town will be humorously diverted, by Punch's celebrated Company of Comical Tragedians from the Hay, who will perform the tragedy of tragedies, being the most comical whimsical tragedy that was ever tragedized, by any tragical company of comedians, called 'The Humours of Covent Garden, or the Covent Garden Tragedy', written by Henry Fielding, Esq. Boxes, 2s.; pit, 1s.; gallery, 6d. [12]

After his nine years as a fair showman, Fielding went on to confound the fanatics who held that all who were associated with the fair bore the taint of the devil. He was one of the few magistrates of the time that took their job seriously, and his work with the Bow Street courts signalled the first attempts to tackle London's crime, leading eventually to the founding of the police force.

Trained animals were always popular at the fair. In the late sixteenth century, a man named Banks had a horse, Morocco, who had extraordinary talents. He 'would restore a glove to the due owner after the master had whispered the man's name in his ear; and would tell the just number of pence in any piece of silver coin, newly showed him by his master'. [13] Banks and Morocco were famous and travelled through Europe, sometimes running into trouble from superstitious people. At Orleans they were accused of devilry by the Capuchins, a charge that could have meant death. Banks told Morocco to approach one of the company with a crucifix in his hat, kneel before him, and kiss the cross. As the devil is supposed to be incapable of approaching the cross, the horse vindicated himself and his master.

A hundred years later, Pepys records seeing a mare that could count money, and the records are full of 'sapient' or 'learned' pigs. Also common were exhibitions of freaks of nature, such as the bull with five legs mentioned in *Bartholomew Fair*. Unfortunately, exhibitors did not draw the line at animals when there was money to be made, and we come to probably the least humane side of fairs. Pepys may have read the newspaper advertising the child born back-to-back with a live bear. This is obviously a fake, and terribly cruel to both child and bear. A few years later in 1701, Brian Fairfax visited May Fair:

> Here was a boy to be seen, that within one of his eyes had DEUS MEUS in capital letters, as GULIELMUS is on a half-a-crown; round the other he had a Hebrew inscription, but this you must take, as I did, upon trust . . .[14]

The taste for human oddities did not abate during the eighteenth century, and is still obvious in William Hone's detailed report of Bartholomew Fair, which he published in 1831. Of the twenty-two shows visited, eight involve some form of human captivity, either dwarfs, giants, red Indians, or Malayan savages. When Hone visited the fair there were already signs of decline:

> The pens immediately contiguous to the passage through them from Bartholomew-hospital-gate towards Smithfield-bars, were not, as of old, decked out and denominated, as they were within recollection, with boughs and inscriptions tempting hungry errand boys, sweeps, scavengers, dustmen, drovers, and bullock-hankers to the 'princely pleasures' within the 'Brighton Pavilion', the 'Royal Eating Room', 'Fair Rosamond's Bower', the 'New London Tavern', and the 'Imperial Hotel': these names were not:—nor were there any denominations; but there was sound, and smell, and sight, from sausages almost as large as thumbs, fried in miniature chipping-pans by old women, over fires in saucepans; and there were oysters, which were called 'fine and fat', because their shells were as large as tea saucers . . .[15]

The only theatre company in evidence at Hone's visit was Richardson's. This well-known company ran throughout the early nineteenth century, at least until 1855 when Bartholomew Fair ended for good, and was a regular visitor to the other annual fairs such as Southwark Fair, or Horn Fair at Charlton. Hone describes a booth thirty feet tall and a hundred feet wide, outside of which a band of ten musicians, all dressed as beefeaters, played clarinets, violins, trombones and a bass drum to attract custom.

The company promised a change of performance each day. The day Hone visited, a melodrama was in performance:

RICHARDSON'S
THEATRE
This Day will be performed, an entire New
Melo-Drama, called the

WANDERING
OUTLAW

Or, the Hour of Retribution
Gustavus, Elector of Saxony, *Mr. Wright.*
Orsina, Baron of Holstein, *Mr. Cooper.*
Ulric and Albert, Vassals to Orsina,
Messrs. Grove and Moore.
etc.
The Piece concludes with the DEATH of ORSINA, and the
Appearance of the
ACCUSING SPIRIT
—followed by

HARLEQUIN

FAUSTUS.

OR, THE
DEVIL WILL HAVE HIS OWN[16]

Nearly a thousand people watched the performance, which featured a variety of painted scenes including a cottage in the forest, a castle, a church and market square, a prison, and a waterfall. However lavish the externals were, though, fair drama was becoming divorced from serious drama, and *The Wandering Outlaw* can hardly be considered in the same class as *The Beggar's Opera*, or *The Cheats of Scapin*.

Hone payed threepence to view a mare with seven feet, which he admitted was genuine, but more popular by this time were collections of exotic beasts, of which there were four in the twenty-two shows visited. Two of these were simply lions, exhibited with very little imagination, but the others were varied and interesting collections. The largest, Atkin's Menagerie, was patronised by George IV and was allowed to display the royal arms. It included a lion mated with a tigress, their hybrid cubs, an elephant trained to pick up coins with its trunk and buy gingerbread, pelicans, condors, monkeys, and an emu. Hone comments that they were all well cared for, which is more than can be said for some of the human exhibits. His levity is misplaced when he comments on an exhibition of a Yorkshire giantess, a Waterloo giant, and an Indian chief: 'The abdication of such an *Indian Chief* as this, in favour of Bartholomew Fair, was probably forced upon him by his tribe.'[17]

The remainder of the shows described included a peep show, consisting of painted scenes viewed through magnifying glasses, a waxworks featuring Mary Queen of Scots, George IV, Othello, Jane Shore (Edward II's mistress) and others, and a glass-blowing exhibition. There was also a fair amount of human talent on show, five companies offering varied programmes of rope-dancing, acrobatics, balancing tricks with swords, or dancing on a running horse, all accompanied by clowns. Brown's Grand Troop From Paris had the additional attraction of a conjuror who gave a boy beer to drink through a funnel, and then caused the beer to flow out of the boy's ears through the same funnel. Finally, one feels the fair would have been incomplete but for the presence of 'Toby, the swinish Philosopher, and Ladies' Fortune Teller'.[18] Hone concludes his colourful stroll through the fair with a rather surprising opinion:

> Bartholomew Fair must and will be put down . . . No person of respectability now visits it, but as a curious spectator of an annual congregation of ignorance and depravity.[19]

The beginning of the end was in 1830, when Lord Kensington, descendant of Sir Richard Rich, sold his interest in the fair to the Court of Common Council. Although Smithfield Market was enjoying record receipts at this period, the show booths were going through a lean period. In 1831 Richardson's lost £50, and Wombwell's Menagerie broke even. The Court deliberately made things more difficult. In 1837 rents were doubled. Wombwell's for example rose to £70. Two years later they went up again, Wombwell's finding they had to pay over £80. In 1840 all shows were banned, with the exception of wild animals and gymnasts. An eyewitness describes the fair in 1854:

> It consisted of a row of stalls which reached from the corner of Windmill Court, Giltspur Street, to the corner of Long Lane, there were three built Gingerbread stalls . . . the rest for Toys, Gingerbread, Wheels of Fortune etc. were open either on barrows or trestles—6 Peep shows, one of which was called a Marionette Theatre—had moving Figures and water works—two Weighing Machines and a Microscope in which was exhibited a flea with a collar and chain completed the fair.[20]

The following year there were no stalls at all. Bartholomew Fair had been suffocated by the Court of Common Council. Of course, plenty of fairs remained for the showmen to frequent, and new 'markets' were developing with the growth of seaside resorts. During the last years of Bartholomew Fair, Henry Mayhew, the great Victorian sociologist, conducted a huge survey of working-class London, including interviews with several street showmen.[21] Interestingly, although several of them thought that street life was getting harder, not one of them even mentioned the decline of Bartholomew Fair.

Mayhew's strolling actor was one of the few showmen who seemed to genuinely like the wandering life, as he said:

> Mummers is the poorest, flashest, and most independent race of men going . . . The generality of them is cobblers' lads, and tailors' apprentices, and clerks . . .[22]

The description given of the strolling troupe has certain similarities with the Italian *commedia*. None of the actors used parts, but improvised around a given character. They had their own form of slang which included fragments from Italian. For example 'My nabs has nanti dinali' meant 'I have no money.'[23] The costumes were more romantic than accurate. In *Fair Rosamond*, Henry II would wear a cavalier costume, while in

Robert, Duke of Normandy the lead actor would wear Turkish trousers, a long cloak, and a hat with feathers. Other plays in the repertoire included *Blue Beard* and two Victorian melodramas, *Maria Martin or the Murder in the Red Barn*, and *The Murder at Stanfield Hall*. Mayhew's actor seemed to think the lack of variety in costume and material did not matter, as each town was only visited once a year. If the visit was in fair time, they would have no trouble from the law, but otherwise a mayor could send them away if he objected to them. The actor once spent a fortnight in gaol for acting without permission. His troupe had set up at Walworth, in South London, and had played unmolested for eleven months, a situation they hoped to sustain by bribing the local policeman with beer and money. But they were finally infiltrated by plainclothes policemen, who arrested everybody in the canvas theatre. One hundred spectators were fined a shilling, while the actors were each fined twenty. Those who could not pay were gaoled for fourteen days. The whole troupe was led through the streets to the court, still in their costumes, and the crowd pelted the police with vegetables. The costumes were kept on during the duration of the sentence:

> I had a long figured chintz waistcoat, and a pair of drab knee-breeches, grey stockings, and low shoes, and my hat was a white one with a low crown and broad brim, like a Quaker's. To complete it, I wore a full bushy wig.[24]

The humour with which this strolling player recounted the story of his imprisonment demonstrated a tremendous zest for the life of the road. This is more than can be said for the Punch and Judy man interviewed by Mayhew. He seemed preoccupied with the decline of his trade, and was convinced that he would die in the workhouse. He claimed to have bought his show from Porsini, a famous Italian showman of the late eighteenth century, for thirty-five shillings. Porsini and Pike his apprentice used to make up to £10 a day, and were comfortably off in their heyday, but both died in the workhouse. By the time of Mayhew's interview, about 1850, Punch's earnings had dropped to an average of £5 a week. To earn this, the showman would have to walk about twenty miles a day carrying the apparatus, pestered by hordes of boys from the East End of London and give maybe twenty shows. Easier takings were from private shows at gentlemen's houses, or on the pavement outside. A party for a nobleman's children might bring in £2 for an hour and a half's work. The problem, the showman said, was not that Punch had been around too long:

> People isn't getting tired with our performances; they're more delighted than ever; but they're stingier.[25]

Figure 10 Punch's showmen

During the summer months, Punch would be out of London, visiting especially the seaside resorts then becoming fashionable. If two shows accidentally met in the same town, they would swap their pipe and drums men, and share the combined takings equally. According to Mayhew's showman, there were sixteen

Punch shows in Britain, each with two men. Eight of these were in London, and eight in the country. They all knew each other, and knew of each other's whereabouts, all co-operating with one another so as not to spoil any pair's pitch. They also had a quasi-Italian slang, similar to the strolling actors'.

The Punch and Judy show (*see* Figure 10) was not always the squeaking, slapstick rough-and-tumble that we know today, although it was possibly beginning to grow like that in the 1850s, when audiences were becoming predominantly infant. Mayhew's man said he used to go to the theatre to learn, and claimed to have added the ghost to the Punch story after being deeply affected by the funeral procession in *Romeo and Juliet*. He also drew a parallel between Punch and Othello, both wife-killers, and saw the outcome as an example to married couples. His description of Punch past is possibly historically inaccurate, and a little confused in its moral sense, but interesting all the same:

> At first, the performance was quite different then to what it is now. It was all sentimental then, and very touching to the feelings, and full of good morals. The first part was only made up of the killing of his wife and babby, and the second with the execution of the hangman and killing of the devil—that was the original drama of Punch, handed to posterity for 800 years. The killing of the devil makes it one of the most moral plays as is, for it stops Satan's career of life, and then we can all do as we likes afterwards.[26]

> Talk of Punch knocking the Fantoccini down. Mine's all show, Punch is nothing and cheap as dirt[27]

—This was the rather aggressive opinion of the *fantoccini* man interviewed by Mayhew. He had puppets two feet tall with fancy costumes, all of which he had carved himself, and a theatre that stood ten feet tall, with a stage height of four feet. He could afford to pay a labourer a guinea a week simply to carry all the equipment around, and he and his piper each earned about £2 a week. Their pattern of work was similar to Punch's, walking around the streets, pitching at crossroads, and hoping for evening engagements at gentlemen's houses. In the summer they would go to the seaside, in particular Brighton. Despite the showman's obvious sense of superiority—he admitted that the common crowd was a great annoyance to him—he seemed to be experiencing a similar recession to Punch. He claimed to have earned £20 a week in past seasons at Brighton, where he was a major attraction:

> I recollect going down with the show to Brighton, and they actually announced our arrival in the papers, saying, that among other public amusements they had the Fantoccini figures from London.[28]

The first man to exhibit the *fantoccini* in the streets in England was a Scotsman called Gray, in the early years of the nineteenth century. In the opinion of Mayhew's man, Gray killed Porsini's Punch trade. He earned £10 a week performing at the Vauxhall pleasure gardens, and also played for George IV. As well as this, he took money in the streets, but how much apparently no one ever found out, 'for he was a Scotchman and uncommon close'.[29]

The attraction with *fantoccini*, or marionettes, was their apparent independence. All the limbs were visible, and they seemed to move them free of human assistance. The performance described by Mayhew's man was a series of dances to music, with such varied characters as Grimaldi, Scaramouche, a sailor dancing a hornpipe, and an 'enchanted Turk', whose limbs flew off and became separate figures. He also had an old lady whose arms turned into figures, and whose body turned into a balloon, in which the figures flew away. Certainly a great deal of ingenuity went into devising and making the figures, but that was possibly part of the reason for the *fantoccini*'s decline. If the public were given something exceptional in the *fantoccini*, then they would expect a continual supply of exceptional novelties, which would be very difficult to sustain. Moreover, despite their ingenuity, the *fantoccini* lacked a central character with whom the public could identify. Punch has a personality of his own that endures today, and this is largely why he has survived. Marionettes are still popular, but not in such a universal way as Mr Punch.

Will Kemp's accompaniment of pipe and drum altered little in two and a half centuries. Whether he was standing outside a conjuror's booth at Bartholomew Fair, or marching into a provincial town at the head of a troupe of acrobats, announcing their arrival with music, the drummer and piper was an essential figure in the world of street entertainment. He was there to turn people's heads, attract custom, and in some cases provide accompaniment to the show offered. Mayhew spoke to one who referred to himself as simply an old street showman. This man's story typified the life style of the opportunist with no particular talent of his own, but a need to keep moving. It was adventurous, varied, at times harsh, and ultimately insecure. He started off as a sweep's boy, a life that was in the early nineteenth century so desperately hard that it is not surprising that he ran away with an organ grinder, playing the pandean pipes for five shillings a week and his keep. He saved enough to buy a drum, and left the organ man for an Italian called Michael, who had a monkey and a dancing bear. Billy the monkey would jump up and down on the bear, Jenny, and hop onto Michael's shoulders, while Jenny would do somersaults and dance round a pole. They also had two dancing dogs, who would jump through hoops and dance on their hind legs. They found the West End of London the most lucrative, while Whitechapel, although good for a crowd, tended to produce mainly halfpennies. Sometimes butchers would set two or three bulldogs onto the bear, which was not an aggressive animal. Although the show would usually take twenty or thirty shillings a night, the drummer and piper's wages were seven shillings a week and keep.

Mayhew's showman considered the provinces better than London for the business, although some places, such as Cheltenham and Gloucester, would not allow them in the high streets, and despite the fact that Jenny's accommodation sometimes caused problems. She was fed on bread, potatoes, and carrots, which vegetarian diet prevented her from becoming savage, and was generally well-behaved, but she did tend to frighten people at the lodging houses where they stayed. Around 1820 they all spent a weekend in prison after playing the day after the end of Chester races. Apparently race meetings had the same custom of toleration of entertainers as fairs, but this overstepping of the privilege had unfortunate results. The bear was shot,

Michael returned to Italy with the lion's share of the takings, and the showman was left stranded in Chester with only his drum and his pipes.

The showman drummed and piped his way from Chester to London, where he joined an exhibitor of clockwork figures. These figures were two feet high, and danced on a table. They had Bluebeard, a Turk who shook his head, rolled his eyes, and waved his sword, a sailor dancing a hornpipe, and Lady Catarina, a fashionable lady who danced a reel. They could expect to earn ten or twelve shillings a time performing in a nobleman's house, and at race meetings £3 was not an unusual day's takings. On average, the showman earned fifty shillings a week clear. When Christmas approached, they would lay up the clockwork figures, and take round a magic lantern, or galanty show. 'It was shown by way of a treat to the scholars. There was Harlequin and Billy Button, and such like.'[30] The magic lantern was the earliest form of slide projector, and a ceiling or sheet was often used as a screen. By the 1850s the demand for these shows was dropping off, as magic lanterns themselves could be bought fairly cheaply. By the time Mayhew interviewed him, the old showman had fallen on hard times again. He had been prosperous with the clockwork figures, and had saved money, but an attack of rheumatic gout had eaten into his savings, leaving him penniless once more. Like Porsini, Pike, and so many others, he probably ended up in the workhouse.

The notion of the melancholy clown is one that often recurs in art, and it is rather sad that both of the street clowns interviewed by Mayhew confirmed it. The first had tried to join the police, amongst other attempts to find an alternative to street clowning, but he seemed resigned to the fact that he would never find a way out of it. Sometimes he would go solo, or sometimes with a group of acrobats or dancers, and his average earnings, to support a wife and three children, were eight shillings and sixpence a week. By comparison, a London docker of the same period might earn an average eleven shillings and tenpence a week, so it was no easy life raising a laugh on the streets. What made it more difficult was the need to appear cheerful, as the clown himself complained: 'Many times I have to play the clown, and indulge in all kinds of buffoonery with a terribly heavy heart.'[31]

He seemed to think that the regular street clowns' trade was being ruined by part-timers, who donned the fool's cap and white make-up on holidays, when the best custom was to be had. He also showed abject pessimism as to his future. Most street clowns he said died in the workhouse, wretched and poverty-stricken, and he did not dare think of what was going to happen to him in his old age. Minutes after this dolorous interview, Mayhew saw the same man in action, 'dancing and singing in the streets as if he was the lightest-hearted fellow in all London'.[32]

The streets of London in the nineteenth century used to witness the sort of scenes we nowadays associate more with the circus. The stilt-walkers in Figure 11 were a family; a mother

Figure 11 Street performers on stilts

and two daughters. They were managed by the father, who used to expect to take £3 at least for an afternoon's work. Of course, they did not restrict themselves to London. The more spectacular acts could travel into Europe, as well as doing the rounds of the English provinces. The specialised training required for some of the feats performed was often passed on from father to son, or mother to daughter. A street acrobat described how he was 'cricked' every morning by his father, to keep his limbs and joints supple:

> He put my breast to his breast, and then pulled my legs up to my head, and knocked 'em against my head and cheeks about a dozen times. It seems like as if your body was broken in two, and all your muscles being pulled out like India-rubber.[33]

By the time he was twelve, this acrobat was performing in French theatres with a troupe. They also pitched in the streets, and at the fêtes of St Cloud, St Germain, St Denis, and Versailles. He seemed to think that the French were more generous than the English. One Sunday he and his companions collected 700 francs, or roughly £28, which was a year's wages for a working man at that time. Playing in France did have its drawbacks, though. In 1848 the acrobats were caught up in the revolution and forced to fight on the barricades in Paris. Four years later they were deported by the Republicans, along with all foreigners, and so returned to pitching in the streets in England.

One of the favourite feats performed by the troupe was known as 'the perch'. One man held a 24ft pole, and another one ran up it, and did various tricks, such as hanging down by one toe with his arms out. From the top of the pole, he could see into first-floor drawing rooms, where people were peeping at the show from behind curtains. Once discovered, people were more likely to make a contribution. Despite the perilous nature of his livelihood, the acrobat said that accidents were rare, except that they often put their hip-bones out, for which they would only be out for a week. If any member of the 'school' did break a limb, the others would continue to give him his share of the takings while he got better. In the winter, the troupe would be hired by a theatre to play in a pantomime. The acrobat explained that this did not require a sudden adaptation towards a different kind of mental concentration:

> We never speak in the play, but just merely rush on, throw somersaults, and frogs, and such-like, and then rush off again.[34]

The street acrobat reckoned on an overall income of £100 a year. His whole tone was more cheerful than some of the street entertainers already mentioned, which could possibly be due to the fellowship involved in travelling with a troupe, and also to the greater security he enjoyed. But it may also be simply because he was still a young man when interviewed, and had yet to come to the harsh periods of responsibility for a family, or the realisation that he would one day be too old to perform.

Figure 12 Street acrobats performing

Lewis Nelson called himself a 'street Risley'. The Risley business was a type of acrobatics or tumbling in which a young lad was thrown from hand to hand, and from hand to foot, while turning somersaults, by an older man. Lewis started off by practising walking on his hands, and tumbling, while still with his parents, who were ordinary working-class people in London. While still a lad he was taken to Norwich with his younger brother, Johnny, by a man who introduced them to the Risley business. The man was cruel to them, so they ran away, Lewis carrying Johnny thirty miles on the first night of their escape. They went back to London, walking all the way, and earning pennies by tumbling. Their parents had been against the entertaining life from the start, but rather than settle down to forget an unfortunate experience, the boys incorporated the middle brother, Sam, into the act, and started working in London. They earned twelve shillings a day performing outside Peter's Theatre at Stepney Fair, doing acrobatics and the Risley business. Lewis would stand with a brother in either hand, throw them into the air in somersaults, and catch them. Then he would lie on a carpet and throw them from foot to foot. Sam was capable of turning up to fifty-five somersaults without stopping, and Johnny twenty-five.

After polishing their act in London, the Nelson brothers went to play the provinces, taking a drummer whom they paid two shillings and sixpence a day and a pot of beer. Their takings varied, but they usually sent at least £1 back to their parents each week. They would often have to ask permission of the mayor before they could play in the streets, and sometimes they found it better to hire a room in which to perform. On one occasion, at Brenford in Norfolk, they had a room full of about a hundred people, when their showy costumes had an unexpected effect on the superstitious rustics:

> When the people see'd me and my brothers come on dressed all in red, and tumble about, they actually swore we were devils, and rushed out of the place . . . We came out with red faces and horns and red dresses, and away they went screaming.[35]

What happened when the Nelson boys grew up we do not know, but the Risley business certainly survived into the twentieth century. It disappeared from the streets, probably because it was appealing enough to be a success in the circuses and music halls which drew in so much talent in the later nineteenth century.

Figure 13 Street conjuror performing

Another entertainer who ran away from his parents was the street juggler interviewed by Mayhew. He had practised tumbling on rubbish heaps in London, but when he saw Ramo Samee, the famous Indian juggler, on the stage, he decided that that was what he wanted to be. He soon broke all the plates at home trying to learn juggling, and had to tumble around public houses to earn enough money for a tin plate and wooden balls with which to practise. He ran away from home with a showman who paid him nothing but his keep. He was glad to do

it at the time, simply because he liked tumbling, but when he
got older and more skilful he set himself up on his own. He had
an Indian outfit made, which seems from the description to have
been a combination of the wide variety of the Orient. He wore
Turkish trousers and waistcoat, a skull-cap, and a long horse-hair
tail hanging down his back. In this costume, calling himself the
'Indian Juggler', he worked his way to Dublin, playing in the
streets, juggling on stilts, and playing his own drum and pipes:

> I played any tune,—any think, just what I could think of, to draw
> the crowd together; then I'd mount the stilts and do what I called 'a
> drunken frolic', with a bottle in my hand, tumbling about and
> pretending to be drunk. Then I'd chuck the balls about, and the
> knives, and the rings, and twirl the plate.[36]

In Ireland he used to raise a laugh by throwing up a raw
potato to smash on his forehead. He was a great success in
Ireland, being a bit of a novelty, and would have been a
prosperous man if he had not married a wife who drank away his
booth, wagon, horse, and all. He returned to England, working
the seaside towns in summer, and playing regularly in London.
He became a well-known figure on Tower Hill in the 1850s, and
the police would apparently turn a blind eye to his performances,
which continued to bring him about £1 a week. By his
estimation there were about twenty street jugglers in England at
that period. Once again, juggling was the kind of skill that
would have found employment in the music halls later in the
century, which partly accounts for the disappearance of jugglers.

The first time we came across the term 'busking' was in the
story told by a street conjuror. He had been the door-keeper at
the Blackfriars Rotunda, until one day the wizard failed to show
up and he stepped in and did the tricks. From then on he started
playing the streets, teaming up with a fire-eater. They used to
perform at public gatherings on holidays. Epsom races for
example was a good bet. Conjuring is a type of performing that
can directly involve the audience, and by approaching the
carriages of the nobility, large takings could be had. He claimed
once to have taken £7 from one carriage alone. Conjuring was
also well suited to busking, which in his day meant going round

tap-rooms and liquor parlours hoping for employment, and not playing in the streets. Playing in parlours was not well received by the managers, and there was a certain technique to avoid being thrown out:

> When I went into a parlour I usually performed with a big dice, three inches square. I used to go and call for a small drop of gin and water, and put this dice on the seat beside me, as a bit of a draw. Directly I put it down everybody was looking at it. Then I'd get into conversation with the party next to me, and he'd be sure to say, 'What the deuce is that?' I'd tell him it was a musical box, and he'd be safe to say, 'Well, I should like to hear it, very much.'[37]

Once the attention of the parlour had been gained, the manager or waiter would not risk annoying his customers by throwing the conjuror out. One establishment where apparently anything went was Mother Emmerson's in Jermyn Street. Here conjurors, jugglers, or singers could busk unmolested, often enjoying the patronage, or at least the free drink, of the Marquis of Waterford. This wild Irish peer would occasionally hire seven or eight cabs, and put fiddlers and other musicians on the roofs, filling the inside with anybody who wanted a ride. Driving the first cab himself as fast as he could, he would lead the procession through the streets, the bands playing as loudly as possible. Any damages would be paid by him.

During the nineteenth century science became less the domain of the fanatical specialist, and more accessible to the educated amateur. Along with this, the desire to partake in some small way of this growing knowledge was a feeling that gripped most people who had a spare penny in their moments of leisure. The men who fulfilled this desire were in a sense related to the mountebanks, in that they made money by pandering to people's need to be let in on a secret, whether the secret was in reality fact or fancy (*see* Figure 14). A tailor called Tregent used to exhibit a telescope in the London streets, charging a penny for a peep at the moon and the planets. His method of drawing custom was the age-old one of arousing the public's curiosity by making a statement contrary to their general beliefs, or better still getting an innocent bystander to make it for him:

Suppose I'm exhibiting Jupiter, and I want to draw customers, I'll say 'How many moons do you see?' They'll answer, 'Three on the right, and one on the left,' as they may be at that time. Perhaps a rough standing by will say, 'Three moons, that's a lie. There's only one, everybody knows.' Then, when they hear the observer state what he sees, they'll want to have a peep.[38]

On 13 October 1856 an eclipse of the moon was visible in London for just over three hours, and there were great queues for Tregent's telescope—247 people viewed the eclipse, averaging slightly less than a minute and a half per person. The takings came to slightly over a pound, but circumstances were exceptional. Very often there was too much cloud to see anything at all, and Tregent claimed he had known periods of three consecutive lunar months when nothing was visible on twenty out of the twenty-eight nights. The only time Tregent

Figure 14 Street telescope exhibitor

ever left London was on the occasion of the fleet being led out of
Portsmouth by Queen Victoria, for which event his telescope
was once again very popular.

In a similar field was the man who exhibited a microscope
daily outside the London Hospital in Whitechapel, and on Westminster Bridge in the evenings. He had been a successful cobbler,
and had served his apprenticeship with a man who was a keen
astronomer, so when his business failed he had a certain amount
of scientific knowledge. More useful, probably, was the
accumulation of scientific jargon which made his accompanying
lectures more convincing. He had six objects on show: a flea, a
human hair, a section of oak, animalculae in water, cheese mites,
and a section of a schoolmaster's cane. He was related to the
mountebanks in that he pretended to superior knowledge, while
in fact he knew very little about the subjects himself. His lecture
on the tubular nature of the human hair is an example:

> . . . the atmosphere, passing down these tubes, suddenly shuts to
> the doors, if I may be allowed such an expression, or, in other
> words, closes the pores of the skin and thereby checks the insensible
> perspiration, and colds are the result.[39]

He regularly took six shillings a day, charging working men a
penny, and often receiving silver from genteel admirers of his
lectures, but he was neither malicious nor a calculating charlatan,
and probably believed every word he said himself.

We end this chapter with a reminder that, despite the March
of Progress, London could still be a desperately inhospitable
place, and the life of the streets was not all easy money for
workshy idlers. Known to the urchins as Shakespeare, an
educated young man who came to London and was unable to
find work found himself living on his wits. He had a passion for
the stage, and would recite passages from plays in the streets and
public houses, barely scraping ten shillings a week. He would
put on false moustaches and, with a stick for a sword, give the
public famous speeches from *Hamlet, Macbeth, Othello,* or *Richard
III.* If he had a companion, they would perform popular vignettes
such as *The Gypsy's Revenge, The Gold Digger's Revenge, The*

Miser, The Robber, The Felon, or *The Highwayman.* He would regularly recite in Commercial Road, in the East End, but he considered the most theatrically inclined neighbourhood of London to be the Walworth Road, which coincidentally was where our strolling player was arrested after an uninterrupted run of eleven months. Leaving aside regional variations in audience, perhaps the street reciter's worst enemy was that other uncertain factor which has always been the bane of street entertainers, the English weather.

Notes to Chapter 6

1 In Hone, Vol. I, Col. 1216.
2 Henry Morley, *Memoirs of Bartholomew Fair* (1859), p. 231.
3 In Hone, Vol. I, Col. 1247.
4 *The Diary of Samuel Pepys,* 29 August 1668.
5 Ibid., 21 September 1668.
6 In Morley, p. 247.
7 Ibid., p. 336.
8 The cloisters of the old priory were the haunt of prostitutes and pimps.
9 *The Observator,* 21 August 1705, in Hone, Vol. I, Col. 1240.
10 In Hone, Vol. I, Col. 573.
11 In Morley, p. 341.
12 John Timbs, *The Romance of London* (1865), Vol. III, p. 80.
13 Sir Kenelm Digby. In City of London Guildhall Library Prints Department, C21–21 manuscript notes.
14 John Timbs, *Walks and Talks About London* (1865), p. 40.
15 In Hone, Vol. I, Col. 1171.
16 Ibid., Col. 1183.
17 Ibid., Col. 1197.
18 Ibid., Col. 1193.
19 Ibid., Col. 1252.
20 City of London Guildhall Library Prints Department, C21–21.
21 Henry Mayhew, *London Labour and the London Poor* (1967), Vol. III, *The London Street-Folk.*
22 Ibid., p. 141. 'Mummers' here means strolling actors, having lost its traditional meaning concerning annual village customs.
23 Ibid., p. 139.
24 Ibid., p. 142
25 Ibid., p. 50.
26 Ibid., p. 49.
27 Ibid., p. 63.

28 Henry Mayhew, *London Labour and the London Poor* (1967), Vol. III, *The London Street-Folk*.
29 Ibid., p. 61
30 Ibid., p. 73.
31 Ibid., p. 119.
32 Ibid., p. 121.
33 Ibid., p. 90.
34 Ibid., p. 94.
35 Ibid., p. 97.
36 Ibid., p. 106.
37 Ibid., p. 109.
38 Ibid., p. 81.
39 Ibid., p. 85.

7

'THE TRANSPARENT OBJECT OF BEGGING' ON TRIAL

During the eighteenth century England, and in particular London, increased in wealth from such factors as trade with the colonies and industrial development. The contrast between rich and poor was enormous. Some families had to live in the street, and for many, street music was simply a means of drawing attention to their poverty, or even of annoying the wealthy in the hope that they would pay them to go away. Figure 15 is a good starting point, as it gives an honest, unromanticised view of the streets of London at the start of the period we are dealing with; squalid, noisy, and overcrowded. It also shows the noise to be a symptom of the ills of English society and not, as a later critic tried to imply, something that came over with the waves of immigrants in the nineteenth century.

Slightly above the level of beggary, the street ballad business was still flourishing. One of the leading publishers at the end of the eighteenth century, still based on the Seven Dials, was Bat Corcoran. The business had lowered its sights somewhat, and could no longer boast a Swift among its authors. Corcoran himself had no illusions as to the standards of his trade:

> The only two men that ever wrote ballads to my fancy, were slender Ben and over-head-and-ears Nick. Ben had a gift at speeches for the prisoners at the Old Bailey. The man saved lives. The rogues of London Juries knew all his turns to a hair. You have heard of Nick; the poor fellow drank himself out at elbows, paid nobody, rowed watchmen, and played the roaring lion everywhere. That was Nick all over, that was genius to a *t*; there's no hope of a man that doesn't do these things. I never gave the least encouragement to a sober decent man in my life.[1]

Figure 15 'The Enraged Musician' by Hogarth, 1741

Sober and decent they may not have been, but they clung together. The ballad markets at the Beggar's Opera public house gave an opportunity for the singers and fiddlers to drink, sing and shout together on a Saturday night. Sadly, by 1825 the establishment had become the Rose and Crown, and the ballad markets had finished.

A well-known ballad singer was blind Jack Stuart, with his dog Tippo. When Stuart died in 1815, all the ballad singing fraternity turned out for his funeral, which was thought worth commemorating in a ballad. There is something rather touching about the spectacle of a train of blind fiddlers and singers, scraping away behind a coffin. The touch of humour that creeps in, along with the lively rhythm of the chorus, makes the scene faintly ridiculous, and adds to the pathos:

Two fiddlers in front took de lead to de grave,
    While Bob and de rest dat was blind,
With myself, Billy Dawson, and old Jemmy Cave,
    Ve made up de chorus behind.
        Sing ri tum ti tum ti

As ve pass'd Gutter Lane, Dyball's fiddle it stops
    Vas it grief made his fingers to fail?
Yes—twas fumbling for something to vipe the big drops,
    And forgot that his coat had no tail.
        Sing ri tum etc.

'Can't you come it melancholy?' says George turning round,
    'Fie, for shame, boys, ye don't keep the tune.'
'But 'tis grief drives me on,' says the lad when he found
    That he played out his part all too soon.
        Sing ri tum ti etc. [2]

George Dyball was also blind, and also had a dog to assist his
act. The dog would give a pitiful whine, and look at spectators
dolefully. If this did not work, it would pick up the box and rub
it against the spectators' knees. Any money thrown into the tin
the dog would immediately pick up and give to Dyball. Dogs
were a common part of a blind musician's livelihood, which is
hardly surprising, as an important side of their usefulness was to
lead their masters. Charles Wood, a blind man with a grind-
organ, had a dog which he claimed to be 'The real learned
French dog, Bob'.[3] Bob wore breeches, a doublet, and a
powdered wig, and apart from dancing to the music, his major
talent seems to have been picking up the money thrown down.
    In Figure 16, the 'canting ship-wrecked seaman'[4] from
Chapter 1 resurfaces. Joe Johnson was a member of the merchant
navy, but was wounded in the Napoleonic Wars, and found
himself incapable of work. Being only in the merchant service,
he was not entitled to a war pension, and no parish would admit
to owing him any relief; so having given his youthful vigour for
King George and England he found himself classed as a vagrant,
with no money and nowhere to go. He became a well-known
figure on Tower Hill, where his favourite song was 'Storm', by

George Alexander Stevens. The model of HMS *Nelson* which he wore on his head not only drew attention to the nature of his disability, but became part of the act. Joe would move his head around, simulating the movement of the ship, and according to one eyewitness would enact in miniature the changing phases of the song:

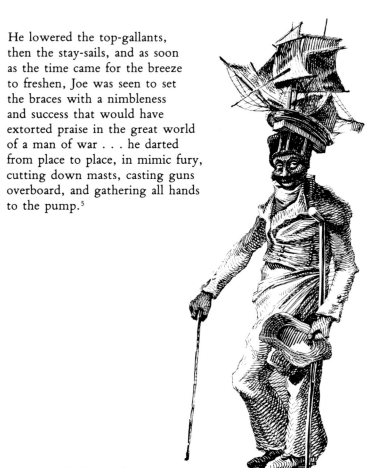

He lowered the top-gallants, then the stay-sails, and as soon as the time came for the breeze to freshen, Joe was seen to set the braces with a nimbleness and success that would have extorted praise in the great world of a man of war . . . he darted from place to place, in mimic fury, cutting down masts, casting guns overboard, and gathering all hands to the pump.[5]

Figure 16 Black Joe Johnson

Joe was also a frequent visitor to the villages surrounding London, such as Staines, Romford, and St Albans. Besides 'Storm', he found other nautical songs such as 'The British Seaman's Praise' and 'The Wooden Walls of England' went down well with a nation imbued with patriotism by the successes of the Royal Navy against the French.

Joe Johnson's inventiveness enabled him to make some kind of living, but there were countless others unable to work, either through illness or war wounds, who were more anonymous and less able to provoke charity. It is true that the nineteenth century saw a great many reformers trying to improve the lot of the lowest members of society. However, it is also true that the middle classes became extremely self-satisfied, and unwilling to contemplate the view that poverty was an inevitable result of the structure of society. For many, street music was the last resort before begging or the workhouse, a fact that seems to have been ignored by its critics in the great public debate of the 1860s. In the preceding decade Mayhew made a comprehensive study of street music in London, which serves as a useful factual backdrop against which to compare some of the claims and attitudes of those who atempted to banish the buskers completely.

This study records about 250 regular ballad singers in London in the 1850s. Many of them went around in pairs, singing comic songs, while the soloists preferred sentimental pieces, such as Byron's popular 'Isle of Beauty'. The pattern was much the same as in earlier centuries, except for the demise of the Saturday-night ballad markets. Publishers were still in the Seven Dials, and singers continued to augment their livelihoods by writing ballads or selling songsheets. The subject matter had altered little too, love, politics and death remaining the favourite themes. Ironically, one of the more popular 'Newgate' ballads, songs supposedly written in prison, was a lament by Calcraft, the hangman, on the decline of his trade. An average ballad singer might hope to make between ten and twelve shillings a week; not much, but enough. Of the 250 regular ballad singers, only a handful were thinly disguised beggars, receiving money out of pity rather than appreciation. Most tried to give some sort of value for money, although the temptation to annoy deliberately with the aim of being paid to shut up was sometimes too strong, as one singer admitted:

> There is a house in Blackfriars' Road where the people has been ill for the last 16 years, and where the street ballad-singer always goes, because he is sure of getting 2d there to move on . . .'[6]

An interesting variety of street singer was the street glee singer. There were many well-trained singers in need of work who felt they were too refined to sing the kind of coarse songs required in the cheap concert halls. Married couples, for example, might call at a gentleman's house and enquire if a short concert was required. In the 1830s a street glee singer might earn £3 a week, but by the 1850s competition was on the increase, and average earnings down to twenty-five shillings a week. This still placed the street glee singer above his vulgar brother in terms of income.

Figure 17 Old Sarah, the well known hurdy-gurdy player

Far more numerous than street singers were street musicians. There were about a thousand of these instrumentalists in London in the 1850s, many of them being down-and-outs and victims of circumstance. Old Sarah (*see* Figure 17) was a blind hurdy-gurdy player who, despite her own poverty, was reputedly cheerful, and is said to have kept 'two or three little pensioners'[7] on her own meagre income. She was born in Drury Lane in 1786, and went blind from an inflammation soon afterwards. She was turned out of blind school because she was not clever with her hands, and sent back to her parents. They died when she was sixteen, and she was sent to the workhouse for four years. There, she was taught a few tunes on the hurdy-gurdy, which had changed little since the Middle Ages. Sarah first learned to play 'God Save the King', and picked up other tunes by imitation. She left the workhouse in 1806 and spent the next fifty years or so on the streets, during which time she had four guides and three instruments. She became a well-known figure, and had a regular round:

> At Kentish-town they calls me Mrs. Tuesday, and at Kensington I'm Mrs. Friday, and so on . . . One maiden lady near Brunswick Square has given me sixpence a week for many a year.[8]

Shortly after her interview with Mayhew, Sarah and her guide Liza were knocked down by a cab—Liza was killed, and Sarah broke both her legs. When she could move again she resumed her round, but because of a crutch she could no longer play, and so was reduced to beggary. Soon afterwards she took to her bed and died.

Many of the poorer street musicians were blind, but not all of them had been blind from an early age. One middle-aged violinist had been a wife and mother, poor but respectable, when blindness struck her at the age of forty-four. Two years later she was widowed and, all her children being already dead, she was forced to sell shoelaces in the street, an activity worth half a crown a week. She was taught the violin by a neighbour, but she was unable to attain any standard of virtuosity, as she admitted:

> . . . I'm not a great performer. I wish I was . . . I get halfpennies in charity, not for my music.[9]

Her income from playing the violin was so uncertain that at times she had to pawn her instrument and revert to selling shoelaces or matches. No doubt her end was just as miserable as Old Sarah's, or any of the countless poor invalids' in the days before the welfare state.

Those who were born blind, and learned music from an early age, often proved to be extremely fine musicians. This was no guarantee though that the streets would offer an easier livelihood. One street harpist had his sight restored when he was nine, by which time he was already a trained musician. He became a teacher of the harp and harpsichord, but took to the streets for lack of custom. He found the streets an inhospitable environment, and complained of constant trouble from boys, encouraged by grown men, pushing and shoving, shouting him down, and cutting his strings. He took about three shillings a week which, with a shilling and a loaf from the parish, just about kept him going. Why the crowd should have been so unsympathetic to him in particular is a mystery. Mayhew describes him as a 'poor, feeble, half-witted, prematurely aged man, dressed in ragged and greasy cloths'.[10] It is possible that his timidity of appearance was one thing that sparked off the scorn of the bullies.

There were several bagpipers who played in the streets of London in full tartan during this period. In the opinion of one Highlander, only five were genuine, the others being Irish pipers using the tartan because of its attractive appearance and romantic associations. He also seemed to think that the Irish, having more cheek, did better at it than the real Highlanders. One of the genuine Scotsmen was an ex-soldier whose eyesight had been damaged after marching in the rain. He was discharged as unfit, and was not entitled to any pension whatsoever, because he had only done ten years' service, and not the required twenty-one. With a wife and family to keep, and unable to work, he took to playing the bagpipes while his daughter danced a Highland fling and the sword dance 'Killim Callam' across clay pipes. He used to take his daughter around the countryside with him, making his way north through the garrison towns, towards Scotland. He could earn about fifteen shillings a week, ten of which he would send to his wife and other children in London. Four hours a day was the most he could manage on the pipes, an extremely strenuous instrument to play. His situation was by no means unique. A piper with the 92nd Highland Regiment had returned from India with only one leg and a family to look after. He made Highland costumes for his children, and they danced to the sound of his pipes. People were usually sympathetic towards genuine cases of distress, especially war invalids, but this hardly made up for the loss of a regular livelihood.

By the mid-nineteenth century Britannia's Empire encompassed the globe, and many of her soldiers could not even speak English. And yet if any of these foreign-looking subjects came to England they were regarded on the whole as aliens and undesirable. In the 1850s there were several tom-tom players trying to earn a living in the streets. One, an Arab, was the son of a British soldier wounded in India. Because the father's papers had been lost in transit, his pension had been held up for six years by the time of the interview, and his son had been obliged to keep him by playing the tom-tom. At first it was a novelty, and brought in as much as eight shillings a day, but eventually takings subsided to an average of three shillings a week. Because of the impossibility of getting food that was untouched by an infidel they had both been forced to desert Islam and become Christians. They had no real desire to be in England, but the service of a foreign Empress had brought them there and left them unable to go home, with no obvious means of livelihood. Once again, their situation was not uncommon. Many British officers serving abroad had native valets, whom they brought back with them. If the officer subsequently died, the servant was faced with the alternative of begging or playing in the streets, and to an Indian the tom-tom was the cheapest and most readily available instrument.

Of course, not all the cases of street music were hard-luck stories. Some, with disabilities, used a little enterprise to improve their lot. One blind man had been performing in the streets for twenty-three years, and had constantly revised his act, as much out of the need for mental stimulation as the hope of increased earnings. He said:

It was always my delight in my leisure moments, and is a good deal so still, to study improvements.[11]

He started off in a street band, earning fifteen shillings a week, but left, complaining that the other musicians could not keep time. He built a cut-down piano onto a chaise, to which he later added bells arranged on a rail, to be played with a leather hammer. His next step was to contrive pedals for the bells, so that he could play the violin simultaneously. Then he built a cello onto a frame, tuned to an open chord, which he bowed with his feet in harmony with his violin. Finally he built four accordions onto a frame, and played them with his feet, while playing the violin with his hands. His earnings averaged fifteen shillings a week which, though nothing handsome, was better than many of his fellows. But much of his well-being lay in the fact that rather than accepting his lot with resignation, he had turned his disability into the *raison d'être* of a lifelong hobby.

One aspect of Victorian London that has disappeared is the use of the Thames as a regular thoroughfare by commuters. There are still pleasure boats taking tourists on trips, but a hundred years ago they were more in the nature of a bus service. Musicians would play on board these boats to entertain the passengers. The boats going west towards Kew had regular musicians, but those starting from Woolwich in the east, steaming up to Hungerford, opposite Westminster, were open to the opportunist. A regular figure on these boats was a lad, fifteen when Mayhew spoke to him, who played a concertina on deck, or in the cabin in winter. The sailors liked the music, and thought it encouraged custom, so they did not object to his presence. In winter, he only worked for three hours until 6pm, most of his custom coming from gentlemen returning home from the office. In summer he would work from midday until 8pm, the pleasure-seekers adding to his business. Apparently, in the 1850s the number of buskers on the penny steamers swelled, and they started to get insolent, so they were banned completely. There were still the fourpenny boats to work on, though, and once the rabble had been discouraged, the better-known musicians were allowed back on the penny boats. The concertina lad was busking six days a week, studying at night school, and also playing at dances three nights a week. His average five shillings a day he handed over to his father, who gave him a few coppers as pocket money.

Around 1850 the St James's Theatre saw the first performances of a man named Pell, who played the bones. He was accompanied by Harrington on concertina, White on violin, Stanwood on banjo, and Germain on tambourine. They all had their faces blacked, and wore costumes similar to those in Figure 18. Soon the streets were full of groups of 'Ethiopian serenaders'. They were known to the public by such names as the Lantum Serenaders, the Ohio Serenaders, or the Kentucky Minstrels, while amongst themselves they were known more prosaically as the Somerstown mob, the King Street mob, or the Whitechapel mob. Some of them were street bands who had changed their style to suit the fashion of the times, while some were just groups of young men jumping on a bandwagon without any real knowledge of music:

> We finished up with the 'Railway Overture', and it was more like the railway than music, for it was all thumping and whistling, for nobody knowed how to play the banjo then.[12]

Figure 18 Ethiopian serenaders

Some of the groups would occasionally play in the cheap theatres at night, or at places like the Ship and Camel in Bermondsey, but most of their work was on the streets. They would sing songs such as 'O, Susannah', 'Going ober de Mountain', or 'Dandy Jim of Carolina'. In between numbers they would throw in a little humorous repartee, like this:

'Did I ebber tell you about that lemoncholy occurrence, Mary Blane, the young girl that died last night in the house that burned down this morning, and she's gone to live in a garret?'
'I shall call and see her.'
'You can't.'
'Cos why?'
'Cos she moved from where she lives now; she's gone to live where she used to come from.'
'Did you ever see her broder Bill?'
'No; he's dead.'
'What, broder Bill dead, too?'
'Yes; I see him this morning, and axed him how he was.'[13]

The police claimed that they were in league with pickpockets. The very fact that they pitched at such places as the Saturday-night markets in Edgware Road, Carnaby Street, or Great Marylebone Street, situations ripe for the pickpockets, would be enough to provoke such allegations. There may well have been some truth in them, although not all of the serenaders were dishonest. Many of them were perfectly willing to make a nuisance of themselves, though:

When we are out pitching, the first place for us is where there is anybody sick . . . We are sure to play up where the blinds are down . . . We don't move for less than a bob, for sixpence ain't enough for a man that's ill.[14]

All the street musicians we have seen so far have been British subjects. However, the nineteenth century saw immigrants from other parts of Europe moving to England. Mid-century England was comparatively prosperous, stable, and peaceful, and the old myth that the streets of London were paved with gold was spreading further afield. Many who came were musicians, and

Plate 3 Ethiopian Serenaders, Greenwich 1884

found playing in the streets a necessity on discovering the myth to be untrue. Mayhew interviewed a German who played in a seven-piece band consisting of three clarinets, two French horns, a trombone, and a saxhorn. The whole band lived in a three-bedroomed flat in Whitechapel, and made a living from the streets and from gentlefolk's parties. In his opinion there were only five German bands in London, totalling thirty-seven musicians, with one or two outfits in the country. There was a certain amount of animosity between the English and German street bands. An English street bandsman complained that the Germans were injuring his trade by undercutting by half. He also claimed that they had completely taken over the Kent and Sussex coasts, ruining the summer trade.

The other major new face on the street music scene was the Italian organ grinder. A ghetto of Italian immigrants developed in Saffron Hill, in the City of London. Mayhew spoke to one who had bought his own flute harmonican organ. It was more usual for a *padrone* or 'godfather' to own several organs, and pay poor families in Southern Italy to send their boys over to England. A *padrone* would pay three or four pounds for a boy, whom he would then set to work with an organ. The boy would get food and lodging, and a few pennies as pocket money. The situation was a helpless one for the boys if the master was cruel or greedy, but Mayhew's man had been well treated, and his master had allowed him to buy his organ from him for £13, giving him eighteen months to pay. The organ had eight tunes. There were a song, a waltz, a hornpipe, a polka, two dancing tunes, and for the more cultured, two pieces from operas such as Verdi's *Il Lombardi*. The tunes were changed once a year, at a cost of ten shillings. The organ grinder had a weekly pattern of visits, going south of the river on a Monday, towards Highbury on a Wednesday, and to Regent Street and Leicester Square on Saturdays. The rest of the week was more haphazard. He had about fifteen houses in Greenwich where he regularly received custom, and all along his regular route were houses where he could usually count on food and drink as well as money. His organ weighed about fifty pounds, and was tiring to carry around all day. The most he had ever made in a day was five shillings at Greenwich Fair, and sometimes his takings were as low as sixpence. By contrast, men who stayed with the *padrone* would receive their keep and fifteen shillings or a pound a month. He did not complain of any trouble with the police, but that was probably because he never gave any trouble:

> The police are very quiet to us. When anybody throw up a window and say, 'Go on', I go. Sometime they say there is sick in the house, when there is none, but I go just the same.[15]

In the 1860s Michael T. Bass MP led a campaign against street music, in which the Italian organ grinder was described as chief villain, with the German brass bands a close second (*see* Figure 19). Street music was regulated by the Metropolitan Police Act 1839, which stated:

That it shall be lawful for any householder within the Metropolitan Police District personally, or by his servant, or by any police constable, to require any street musician to depart from the neighbourhood of the house of such householder on account of illness of any inmate of such house; or of other reasonable cause; and that every person who shall sound or play upon any musical instrument in any thoroughfare near any house, after being so required to depart, shall be liable to a penalty of not more than forty shillings, and in default of payment to be imprisoned for any period not exceeding one month.[16]

There were several drawbacks to the wording of the Act. Firstly, the word 'thoroughfare' excluded such places as mews or cul-de-sacs from the protection of the law. Secondly, the phrase 'other reasonable cause' was in effect worthless. In 1859 Sir Richard Mayne, Chief Commissioner of Police, sent out an order to superintendents, by which constables were forbidden to act against a street musician if any other reason besides illness was given. If a householder had another 'reasonable cause', the constable was to report to the police station, and take advice from an inspector or superintendent. By the time any decision could be taken, the busker could be miles away. A third drawback was that only a householder could make an objection against a busker. Finally, for an arrest to be made, a busker had to play within view of a policeman, after a householder had once asked him, for a reasonable cause, to stop. So all a musician had to do was to stop playing when a policeman was fetched, and nothing could be done to him.

The case of Antonio Capatali exemplifies how ineffective the law was. A barrister, J. F. Stanford, was at home in Langham Place, in Marylebone, engaged in literary occupation, when Capatali's organ disturbed him. Capatali left when Stanford asked him to, but reappeared on the other side of the house. Stanford asked a constable to arrest the Italian, who grew violent. The following day in court, the magistrate Mr Knox conceded that Stanford had given a reasonable cause to ask Capatali to go away, but ruled that, as the prisoner had been sitting on his organ, and not playing it, when the constable arrived, he had been wrongfully arrested. Mr Knox said the correct procedure would have been for Stanford to have taken out a summons against Capatali. He discharged the prisoner, but granted a summons against him. When Capatali reappeared he was acquitted because he had been wrongfully arrested, and Stanford was persuaded to withdraw his charge, as he was himself liable to a charge of wrongfully giving into custody. Mr Knox sympathised with Stanford's case, and actually wrote to Sir Richard Mayne, asking for a plainclothes policeman to be stationed in Langham Place, to get round the loophole of the offence's needing to be in view of a police officer. Despite this preferential treatment, Stanford gained little satisfaction from the whole affair. In May 1864 he wrote to Bass:

> After Antonio Capatali's case, I had a little respite from these abominable organ grinders. They have begun again, however. On Monday, before twelve o'clock, I had three organ-men, besides a brass band of five German lads, whose instruments were all out of tune.[17]

THREE CHEERS FOR BASS AND HIS BARREL OF BEER, AND OUT WITH THE FOREIGN RUFFIAN AND HIS BARREL-ORGAN!

Figure 19

Stanford subsequently obtained a warrant for the arrest of Carlo Congini, but he could not be traced. It was often the case that the *padrone* would send an organ grinder on the country tramp for a while if he had been in trouble.

Bass received scores of letters from indignant sufferers, which he published along with the newspaper reports and police reports as part of his campaign to change the law. The picture his book gives is of a London completely overrun by a plague of Italian organ grinders, aided and abetted by the lower classes. On 4 May 1864 J. E. Hall, who lived near Hyde Park, wrote:

> Opposite to my house lodges a person who pays organs. I have asked her not to do it. She persists in doing it. I order off the organ man: he refuses to go. I seek a policeman—the lodger stands on her balcony, and long before a policeman can reach the spot, she gives the musician notice, who disappears.[18]

Bass did have a genuine case. Many of his letters were simple complaints from professional men who found it difficult to pursue their livelihood because of interruption from the noise outside. James McConechy, curate of St Paul's Temporary Church at Campden Hill, Kensington, said that the laity were complaining to him at the quality of his sermons. He claimed that, although he began his study and preparation on a Tuesday, he was so interrupted by organs that the laity were lucky to get anything at all like a sermon on the following Sunday. Music was another profession that tended to suffer from buskers, as William Callcott complained:

> I am a professor of music; my work is very often seriously interrupted by the street-organ nuisance. Indeed, I am frequently compelled to relinquish altogether my professional avocations, and lay them aside until the noise is over.
>
> I beg to forward you a memorial, signed by the leading musical professors in London, and also by the pianoforte-*tuners*—a class whose work is entirely stopped when street music is going on.[19]

Other musicians and composers wrote complaining that German bands played deliberately out of tune in an attempt to offend the ears of the professionals. Some suggested that they were particularly sequestered because it was known that their occupations required concentration. Amongst the leading Victorian figures supporting Bass was Charles Dickens:

> Your correspondents are, all, professors and practitioners of one or other of the arts or sciences. In their devotion to their pursuits— tending to the peace and comfort of mankind—they are daily interrupted, harassed, worried, wearied, driven nearly mad, by street musicians. They are even made especial objects of persecution by brazen performers on brazen instruments, beaters of drums, grinder of organs, bangers of banjos, clashers of cymbals, worriers of fiddles, and bellowers of ballads; for, no sooner does it become known to those producers of horrible sounds that any of your correspondents have particular need of quiet in their own houses, than the said houses are beleaguered by discordant hosts seeking to be bought off.[20]

The letter was also signed by Alfred Tennyson, John Everett Millais, W. Holman Hunt, Wilkie Collins, and twenty-three other lesser-known eminent Victorians. It was true that many of the musicians went out of their way deliberately to annoy, and knew how to pick their moment. A gentleman signing himself 'Paterfamilias' wrote to *The Times*, complaining of the interruption of his daughter's piano lessons, which she received twice weekly from a well-known pianist. He claimed that the tutor's arrival was regularly followed by the appearance outside of a band of five blind men—two clarinets and three cellos— called the 'Scotch Crawlers'. After paying them to go away he would be pestered by a succession of acts, such as the 'notorious widow, whose infant phenomena perform irritating sonatas on a jingling pianoforte placed on a costermonger's vegetable truck, drawn by a small donkey'.[21] The scene reminds one of Hogarth's 'The Enraged Musician' (*see* Figure 15).

With this arsenal of evidence, it seems surprising that Bass could anticipate any opposition to his campaign. But Lord Fermoy and John Shelley, Members of Parliament for Marylebone and Westminster, were opposed to the abolition of street music, and it was in their constituencies that any change in

Figure 20 'Southwark Fair' by Hogarth

the law would have had most effect. The fact was the organ grinders were popular with common people, and the tone of some of the letters to Bass shows an element of snobbishness. Charles Aston Collins, who was fortunate enough to live in Hyde Park Gate, wrote:

> The abolition of street music is most earnestly desired by a large body of the inhabitants of London. Its retention is desired probably by a still larger section, but one really of comparatively little importance.[22]

His neighbour, J. Hall, seemed to think that Fermoy and Shelley were playing for popularity in forwarding 'the old claptrap argument of the rich interfering with the amusements of the poor',[23] and dismissed the idea peremptorily:

> The argument that servants like it is not worth notice, for surely the law is not to be accommodated to them, to the sacrifice of those who feed, house, and pay servants.[24]

Punch was most outspoken in support of Bass's campaign. It was very much a voice of the middle classes, reactionary, complacent, and tending to reaffirm the kind of thinking by which a man might see himself as 'Paterfamilias'. It painted the Italians in blackest terms, as Figure 19 illustrates, with the German brass bands as vice-culprits. This was symptomatic of the self-righteous complacency of the section of society for which it wrote. By attempting to foist the blame onto foreign immigrants, it refused to admit that there was anything wrong with British society. The parallels drawn between the music lessons at the house of Paterfamilias and the engraving by Hogarth, executed at a time when the Italian organ grinder was a stranger to London, demonstrate that the problem was indigenous. There were hundreds of English people who either could find no work, or were disabled, and they were out in the streets starving while Paterfamilias reclined in luxury. 'Mr Gladstone's Morning Concert', which appeared in *Punch* on 25 June 1864, is typical of the way the magazine supported the campaign:

A concert was given yesterday morning to the Right Hon. the CHANCELLOR OF THE EXCHEQUER, in front of his private residence at Carlton Terrace. The entertainment commenced by a vocal and instrumental performance of nigger-minstrels, who executed a variety of national airs. The programme included:—

'Polly Perkins'..........................SNOBSON
March from *Faust*.......................GOUNOD
'The Young Man from the Country'.......GENTKINS
'The Dark Girl Dressed in Blue'...........BEEST
'Still so Gently'........................BELLINI
Sestet—'We've got no Work to do'.........CADGERS
Fantasia on Violin......................BLOKE
Recitative—'My Christian Friends'.........MUMPER
Pot-Pourri ....LANDLAUFER

The first five pieces of the foregoing list were performed on the grinding organ by SIGNOR SPORCHINI of Genoa and Saffron Hill, who encored himself several times. CADGERS'S popular invocation of public charity was characteristically rendered by a party of singers in white aprons, who personated mechanics out of employ; a lot well known to the police. The fantasia of that obscure composer, BLOKE, was interpreted by MR. MILLBANK in his usual style; and the blind man's Appeal 'My Christian Friends' was effectively delivered by BAMFIELD. A German band performed LANDLAUFER'S medley of polkas, waltzes, and overtures, and did, in every respect, full justice to the composer's name.

The effect produced on MR. GLADSTONE, by the performances above specified, in regard to street music, was, it is said, a determination to support instead of opposing MR. BASS'S Bill for the abatement of that nuisance.[25]

As well as attacking immigrants, the campaign criticised the taste of the people who encouraged the nuisance, using such epithets as 'vulgar' and 'coarse'. Some of Bass's supporters believed that street music could be discouraged by *Punch*'s cartoons making the lower classes ashamed of their vulgarity in liking a type of entertainment that the more refined despised. This particular aspect of the campaign was deservedly doomed to failure. But it is dangerous to use such terms as 'reactionary' and 'complacent' about a cause supported by a man like Dickens, who spent his whole life trying to jolt Victorian society out of its complacency, and to sit up and notice the poor. Mayhew has shown us that many street musicians were genuinely helpless cases, and also that many of them were gentle, harmless characters, who would never cause the kind of disturbances described by *Punch* and Bass. However, there were abuses, and in these cases the law as it stood was wholly inadequate to protect the persecuted householder.

One householder who seems to have had a particularly hard time was Charles Babbage. He was a mathematician and writer, and did much of his work at home. In 1864 he published *Passages from the Life of a Philosopher*, which included 'A Short Chapter on Street Nuisances'. In this he described, in an exasperated tone, his experiences with street musicians during the few years leading up to Bass's Bill. Between 3 July 1860 and 1 May 1861 he kept a tally of interruptions, which included ninety-six visits by organ grinders, nine by brass bands, and sixty by other unspecified street musicians. He worked out that this deprived him of one quarter of his working potential. He also computed that 4.72 per cent of the population of London was ill at any given moment, which meant that in the street where he lived, Manchester Street, just north of Oxford Street, there were a constant twenty-six invalids, who would suffer from the street musicians. It did not occur to him that the percentage was as high as 4.72 per cent because people who lived in slums a long way from Manchester Street, who could not afford decent nutrition, would be far more likely to fall ill than his neighbours. But this blinkered philanthropy was typical of the time.

During one year Babbage spent nearly £104 on legal costs, prosecuting mainly unsuccessful cases against street musicians who refused to go away. This sum was equivalent to a year's wages for a skilled workman. Babbage's persistence finally won him some convictions, but the reaction to this showed that he was plainly in a minority amongst his neighbours. Placards abusing him appeared in shop windows the whole length of Manchester Street, from Edgware Road to Tottenham Court Road. Because he had taken steps against street musicians, he became a target for their persistent annoyance, and many people who enjoyed not only the music but also the opportunity to infuriate their social superior joined in. Babbage indignantly complained of:

> . . . a perverse disposition of some of my neighbours, who, in two or three instances, have gone to the expense of purchasing worn-out or damaged wind instruments, which they are incapable of playing, but on which they produce a discordant noise for the purpose of annoying me.[26]

He also complained of anonymous threats through the post, broken windows, and offensive objects such as dead cats being thrown into his garden. He claimed that a workman who inhabited an attic overlooking his garden had the habit of leaning out of his window and playing a penny tin whistle for half an hour in the evenings, regularly, with the sole purpose of annoying him. Babbage continued to fight against the street musicians, and if a busker should refuse to go away, he would usually fetch a policeman. He would often be followed as he went by a mob of about a hundred people, shouting abuse at him. He described the mob:

> When I turn round and survey my illustrious tail, it stops; if I move towards it, it recedes; the elder branches are then quiet—sometimes they even retire, wishing perhaps to avoid my future recognition. The instant I turn, the shouting and the abuse are resumed, and the mob again follow at a respectful distance.[27]

Babbage advocated banning street music, and all other noises 'with the transparent object of begging', completely, and suggested that similar treatment should be given to children's tin whistles, hoops, and other toys that might cause a nuisance.[28] In fact, the final outcome of the campaign was far less sweeping than that. In July 1864 *Punch* announced with triumph that Bass's street music Bill had been passed, but in reality all it amounted to was a few alterations to the wording of the existing law. A householder could now use 'the interruption of the ordinary occupations or pursuits of any inmates'[29] as a pretext for requiring a street musician to move on. The amendment also made it easier for an annoyed householder to have the offending musician arrested:

> . . . it shall be lawful for any constable belonging to the Metropolitan Police Force to take into custody without warrant any person who shall offend as aforesaid, provided that he shall be given into custody by the person making the charge and provided also that the person making a charge for an offence against the Act shall accompany the constable who shall take into custody any person offending as aforesaid to the nearest police station-house, and there sign the charge sheet kept for the purpose.[30]

The outcome was about as fair as both sides could hope. While the street musician was not banned out of hand, the householder was given some protection against the kind of persecution experienced by Babbage and Stanford. The real triumph was for democracy. Street music had been spared because enough people had liked it to make a sufficient opposition to the self-important grandees. The whole affair demonstrated that street music survived not only through the enduring charity of the soft-hearted, but also because it provided an entertainment for which there was a considerable demand among the people of London.

Notes to Chapter 7

1   *The Mirror*, 9 July 1825.
2   Ibid.
3   John Thomas Smith, *Vagabondiana* (1817), p. 29.
4   *See* p. 12.
5   *The Mirror*, 9 July 1825.
6   In Mayhew, p. 196.
7   Ibid., p. 159.
8   Ibid., p. 160.
9   Ibid., p. 162.
10   Ibid., p. 174.
11   Ibid., p. 161.
12   Ibid., p. 191.
13   Ibid., p. 192.
14   Ibid., p. 193.
15   Ibid., p. 177.
16   M. T. Bass MP, *Street Music in the Metropolis* (1864), p. 1.
17   Ibid., p. 50.
18   Ibid., p. 10.
19   Ibid., p. 28.
20   Ibid., p. 41.
21   Ibid., p. 67.
22   Ibid., p. 33.
23   Ibid., p. 28.
24   Ibid., p. 29.
25   *Punch, or the London Charivari*, 25 June 1864.
26   Charles Babbage, *Passages from the Life of a Philosopher* (1864), p. 350.
27   Ibid., p. 349.
28   Ibid., p. 359.
29   Metropolitan Police Act 1864, in *Jowitt's Dictionary of English Law* (2nd edition, John Burke 1977), Vol. 2, p. 1213.
30   Ibid.

8

TWENTIETH-CENTURY BUSKERS

The twentieth century has seen many traditions wiped out, and many others placed on the list of endangered species. As we have so far treated this book as a history with some sense of continuity, it is now our job to link what we see today to what we have learned about the past. This chapter is about the twentieth century, which began oddly enough in 1900, not in 1980, and it would be foolish to jump more than a hundred years without even a glance at the passing aspects of street entertainment that have occurred in a century that has seen more drastic and quicker changes than any other.

The beginning of the century saw a tradition of street entertainment virtually unscathed by Victorian attempts to legislate against it. The barrel organ, the *bête noir* of Bass's crusade, was ubiquitous and popular. Several reputable London firms would hire out instruments that were in good working order, with the latest tunes, at a daily rate. People could have them for their own entertainment, or as a means of exploiting an occasion such as a wet Bank Holiday, when there were large captive audiences crying out for the purveyors of gaiety. The barrel organ had ceased to be an exclusively Italian phenomenon. Observers writing for George Sims' monthly magazine *Living London*, which ran from 1903 to 1905, do not even mention the nationality of any barrel organists, which indicates that the instrument had become accepted as part of English life.

The other major target on the Bass–*Punch* hit-list in the 1860s had been the German brass bands. The attitude of *Living London* towards these groups was much more liberal, and appreciative of the musical merit of the performers. The magazine placed German bands high in the aristocracy of street performers, and considered certain anonymous cornet players to be musicians of note. Plate 6 shows one of these brass bands performing in the streets, possibly playing 'The Blue Danube', 'Les Marsellaises' or some other tune of the moment.

During the latter half of the nineteenth century theatre-going had risen greatly in popularity. This does not compare with the Elizabethan and early Jacobean period of theatre-going, when a large proportion of the population of London regularly went to the theatre to watch sophisticated drama that was written to be appreciated at different levels by different mentalities. By this time serious drama was the preserve of the better-educated. While a costermonger of 1600 would have gone to see Shakespeare's *Antony and Cleopatra*, it is doubtful whether three hundred years later George Bernard Shaw's re-dramatisation of the same story can have attracted many dockers or labourers. There were now theatres to cater for all tastes and incomes; music halls where working-class people could hear their own kind of popular song, and witness feats of strength or dexterity performed by strong men, jugglers and acrobats. There was light operetta, Gilbert and Sullivan for those with polite tastes and no head for heavy drama, or full-blown opera. There was serious theatre, with Shaw attempting to provide an alternative to the sterile and stylised Victorian melodrama, suggesting new ideas about society and the *enfant terrible* of political thought, socialism, in a language that could be understood by the less erudite. And there were queues—captive audiences, full of people on an evening out, already in the frame of mind to be entertained and spend money. Busking to queues is essentially a twentieth-century phenomenon, and is one of the very few positive developments in the area of street entertainment that this erasive century can boast.

While new pitches were developing in the West End, the more traditional aspects of street life still retained a great deal of vigour in 1900. In the East End, in the open-air markets of Brick Lane and Whitechapel High Street, as well as in parts of South London, there was an element of the fair in the streets. Kerbstone sellers were the poorest tradesmen, without business premises. Standing with one foot in the gutter and one on the kerb, they sold fruit, newspapers, bootlaces, studs, books, boots, or penny toys. Next to them were ballad singers, harpists, or blind fiddlers, who entertained the everyday working people in their lunch break, or on their way home. Plate 4 shows a blind harmonium player who used to sing hymns by the side of the road. Alongside these timeless figures were shooting galleries, try-your-strength machines, weighing chairs, and even swing boats and merry-go-rounds. Entertainers of a more specialised type sometimes spilled out from the music halls. On stage Arthur Watts styled himself as an equilibrist, but on the streets he was simply called a bottle-carrier. His act involved balancing large wheels and bottles on his head and he had a professional calling-card on which he claimed to be champion wheel- and bottle-carrier of the world. Alongside him, competing for patronage, were street boxers, duets of burlesque pugilist mime in fanciful costumes, posturing to the music of the piano-organ, or pianola. As well as the simply unusual, there were those sights which tried to mix humour with pathos. *Living London* reports a one-legged man dancing in the streets of Whitechapel, and also a man with no legs at all performing a clog dance with his hands to the music of the piano (we are left to suppose that he either

Plate 4 Blind harmonium player, 1905

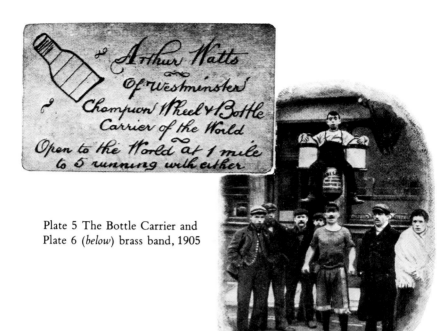

Plate 5 The Bottle Carrier and
Plate 6 (*below*) brass band, 1905

played the piano with his chin, or had an assistant). The disabled have always featured among street entertainers, and have tended to draw down the accusation that street music is simply a noise designed to draw attention to misfortune. But there have also always been people ready to turn their misfortune into a positive value, people like Joe Johnson the disabled seaman, and one must credit their sort, including these two dancers, with a great deal of courage. A one-legged dancer must realise that while half the laughter he provokes may be sympathetic, the rest will be malicious, as human misfortune has always been a great crowd-puller. For this reason, centuries of street entertainers have included those who, considering themselves unfortunate enough to have been born able-bodied, have felt compelled to try to injure themselves in public. Fire-eating is an age-old profession, and is no stranger to the streets of London, but William Ryan, writing for *Living London*, seemed to think that at the turn of the century a profession closely related to fire-eating was the most popular means of endangering one's health. He reported numerous artistes who would bring a table laid for one, perform a short routine of jokes and repartee with the crowd, and then sit down to a meal of pebbles, nails, or broken glass. There were also people who would batter their heads against brick walls, or allow themselves to be punched in the face for sixpence. The lowest of these hard men can hardly be called travelling showmen. They were more in the nature of local toughs, with the desire to make a bit of cash out of their reputations. But they emphasise the fact that in 1905 the life of a community was still in its streets, and that is something that has virtually disappeared in the ensuing three-quarters of a century.

After the First World War a marked change came over the entertainment world. In 1910 there had been a few cinemas in Britain, showing silent films. Fifteen years later virtually everybody went to the cinema every week. The Hollywood dream factory was approaching its peak of production, churning out film after film, promising escape to a fantasy world for a few hours, from the realities of the great Depression. There was a corresponding decline in the music halls, which one by one went out of business, throwing musicians, jugglers, strong men, and clowns onto the streets. The new cinemas provided queues to busk to, but it was small compensation for the loss of a regular livelihood, and as the Depression deepened, times got harder. With seven million people out of work, many amateur musicians turned to busking as a last resort, and the increased competition, combined with the lack of money about, meant it was a hard life. In 1922 another development had created difficulties for street musicians. The BBC began regular broadcasts of radio programmes. Mass media were beginning their takeover of the minds of the people. People could now stay in and be entertained by stars of national fame, instead of having to go out in the cold or wet. Of course, life had always been hard for the street performer, and the most resilient survived. The Boho Brothers (*see* Plate 7) were a well-known band, and probably fared much better than countless disabled ex-servicemen with mouth organs or accordions, but there is something infinitely sad about their smiles.

An act still remembered by many people was Wilson, Kepple and Betty. They began in 1928, at concert parties in seaside

Plate 7 The Boho Brothers, from *Picture Post*, 3 December 1938

towns. Every seaside town had a park or gardens, with or without a bandstand, which the council would hire out to performers for a cut of the takings. The well-off would be charged a penny, and the poor would contribute what they could afford when the hat came round. Performers would do maybe four shows a day. Ken Wilson, with his wife Betty, and Kepple, supposedly Ken Wilson's sister-in-law, became famous with their sand-dancing act. They would throw sand on the stage, or street, and dance in a snake-like way, supposedly after an Ancient Egyptian fashion. The sand was thrown down as a visual gimmick, and they would wear sandpaper on the soles of their shoes to increase the noise of their shuffling. Dressed in red and white striped blazers and straw boaters, they became a popular act on the variety stages in the 1930s. They were soon joined by an addition to the show. Ken junior first went on the stage at the age of four, and grew up in showbusiness. But even a well-known and successful act like Wilson, Kepple and Betty saw hard times in the Depression, and when there was no work at the theatres, they played in the streets.

During the Second World War entertainment was important to keep up people's morale. Wilson, Kepple and Betty played in variety halls alongside such famous artistes as Vera Lynn. There was a syndicate of seven theatres: the East Ham Palace, the Walthamstow Palace, the Metropolitan, Edgware Road, the Shepherds Bush Empire, the Queen's Poplar, the Wood Green Empire, and the Camberwell Palace. They played this circuit during the war, as well as visiting theatres in the provinces.

Besides playing in regular showbusiness, there were still fairs and carnivals to visit annually. Goose Fair in Nottingham still takes place, as do Widecombe Fair on Dartmoor and a host of other less famous fairs whose names are not immortalised in folk songs or stories. When there was no work in the theatres, the Egyptian sand dancers would take their sand and throw it on the ground at a provincial fair.

After the war, Wilson, Kepple and Betty continued to play on the boards and in the streets, but with competition from imitators. A group called the Happy Wanderers became a regular feature at Leicester Square. Albert Hollis, a tap dancer, with two other men and a woman playing the accordion, used to give their version of the sand dance. Their costumes were slightly more oriental, including long striped kaftans, a fez each, and false moustaches. As the north side of Leicester Square became a pedestrian precinct only in the mid 1970s, and the Happy Wanderers used to do their act in the middle of the road there, they were liable to be moved on or fined for obstruction fairly frequently.

The Happy Wanderers shared their name with, or had it stolen by, a band of jazz musicians who used to play in Oxford Street. The band were all ex-servicemen who had been in army bands. Vic and Arthur Stahl played banjos, George Franks, the leader, played the trumpet, Ginger Longman played the trombone, and the band also had drum and clarinet at times. They were all good musicians, and occasionally were hired to play at extravagant parties. They were once flown out to France in a specially chartered aeroplane just for a party, and were given £100 each cash afterwards. But most of their living was made in the streets, where money did not flow quite so readily.

Another sand-dancing act was the Road Stars. Ronnie Ross and Charlie decided that the best effect could be had if they dressed like Whitehall civil servants, with bowler hats and rolled umbrellas, and, of course, false moustaches. Their act finished in 1965, and was the last. The old originals, Wilson, Kepple and Betty, retired in 1960, although Ken Wilson junior continued to play the saxophone in the streets. An old street musician who knew them told us that they retired because they were 'pulled' too many times by the police, and the fines became too much. Another old performer said it was because around 1959–60 the variety halls began to close because of the increase in the number of night clubs and what we now call discotheques.

Technology is a dangerous toy which mankind has not yet learned to use without hurting itself. It is the great destroyer of traditions, and street musicians alongside all the other small men or concerns have had to struggle against its tide. It has brought material wealth to millions, but has also brought serious side-effects to our natural and social environments. At the start of this century *Punch*, steadfast champion of conservatism, had turned

Plate 8 Stanley contemplates while Leoni plays, from *Picture Post*

his pencil against a new threat, and was using the same rather ineffective technique that he had tried against the patrons of barrel organs, that of making the culprits feel ashamed of their own vulgarity, to keep the motor car off the roads. King Cnut can scarcely have attempted a more futile gesture. Now our cities have been completely transformed to serve this particular invention. Communities have been bulldozed to make room for roads, and the existing streets have become environments hostile to humans. Whitechapel High Street is now part of the main lorry route to the Channel ports, and apart from the dangers in crossing the road, the high levels of lead and carbon monoxide make it a place to get through rather than a place to be.

Other technological advances have had adverse effects on all live entertainers, on the stage as well as the streets. Cinema and radio were just the start of an alteration in the pattern of entertainment. They were followed by the television, which enabled people to have a whole evening's entertainment, visual as well as audible, without setting foot outside their own doors. 1960 is a salutary date, as the same year that saw the retirement of Wilson, Kepple and Betty opened a decade in which the rate of change in social conditions accelerated. During the 1960s living standards rose, and television became a part of every household. Record-players also came within the means of ordinary people, and popular music was something that one bought on a plastic disc. Groups like the Beatles and the Rolling Stones captured the imagination of the nation, and the world, like no other groups before them. In 1963 the Beatles' song *She Loves You* had been heard in every part of the country only a few weeks after it had been written. The record industry became one of Britain's biggest exporters, and more money was ploughed back into developing more sophisticated recording techniques. Recorded music began to replace live music in public places. Discotheques became popular, because a record could guarantee a standard of reproduction that an amateur or semi-professional band could not. Even pubs turned to juke-boxes or even to pre-recorded cassettes of music churned out in studios designed to create a sound that was smooth but was totally lacking in flair.

By the end of the decade people who were worried about the obliterative effect of progress on our culture and environment had started to organise themselves. The most extreme, who in the nineteenth century would have called themselves pre-Raphaelites, were hippies, who simply opted out of the mass-production, media-conscious society that most people find themselves part of. Others concerned themselves with ecology, attempting to draw attention to the way economic man ravages the natural world. Specialist groups cropped up too, preservation societies for things such as steam engines, real beer, or even folk traditions such as morris dancing. There was an inevitable backlash in music too. Certain pubs promoted live music, and in 1977 the punk revolution brought a wave of do-it-yourself record companies, preferring the immediacy and vigour of The Clash to the refinement of groups like Pink Floyd, who have been known to spend over a year recording forty minutes of music. But live music's reaction to hypertechnology scarcely affected the street musician. Those pubs which did re-admit live music became fiercely contested venues for bands with reputation and management. One might ask why there was no Campaign to Save Busking. Why are there no Busking Festivals, frequented by hordes of loutish, bearded students, singing 'The Persé owt of Northombarland and a vow to God made he' in an attempt to feel ethnic? Why do the Sunday colour supplements not have advertisements for T-shirts saying 'Keep Music on the Streets'?

In fact, the press have given a lot of publicity to street music in the last two decades, which could be seen as a campaign of sorts. It had begun in 1903 with George Sims' *Living London*. Mayhew's research in the last century was purely for scientific, sociological purposes, but there are some of the qualities of a tourist's guide book about the glossy pages of *Living London*. The East End was an area where most middle-class Londoners would never go, and in late Victorian times not even cabs would venture east of Aldgate. Although Sims has the advantage of the camera over Mayhew, Mayhew had won the confidence of the people he spoke to, and it shows in the result. *Living London* has the effect of trying to put something living into a museum show-case, for people to observe without getting their fingers or their feet dirty. In more recent times a lot of publicity has been given to street music in the newspapers, in glossy magazines, and on television, and it is on the whole sympathetic. Some journalists are genuinely concerned about the disappearance of street musicians from the streets, for reasons such as, among others, police harassment. But to do a colour feature or a ten-minute television film about buskers is to package for the middle-class and comfortable something that they can come out and find for themselves if they really want to. This book is in a sense part of

Plate 9 Frank Bates does a paper-tearing act, from *Picture Post*

that process of defining and packaging. We are not implying that this sort of publicity does any actual harm to street music, except that it is part of the system of living that keeps people at home in their own living-units, rather than out mixing with other people. The point we are making is that no campaign by middle-class observers who perceive that busking is a 'Good Thing', and therefore deserves preservation, can be responsible for perpetuating a tradition that endures through the human qualities that have always made it. The tradition lives on in the men and women that have the same urges that Widsith or Watier had. This century has seen an alteration in the street musician's place in society. Whereas before he was out in the middle of the street, in the forefront of people's consciousness, now he is more of a peripheral figure, an accessory to the overall scene. But he has adapted to the changing environment. The car has invaded his natural environment, so he has created another one in the Underground stations. When his audiences were stolen by the cinema, he played to them while they queued.

One man who has lived through much of the change in this century, and is still going at the age of sixty, is known as Roy, or Little Legs. The fact that he is a dwarf meant that he was more likely to prosper in showbusiness than anywhere else, and he first performed at the age of thirteen, in 1933. His first part was as the dog in *The Babes in the Wood*, at the Palace, Richmond. Then he started to tour concert parties with a comic act, Bert and Billy Betts. The promoter, J. D. Robertson, would contact a town council and arrange to hire the bandstand in the park for a proportion of the takings. Roy would take part in the action, and once people were laughing he would 'bottle'. His stature and quick backchat make him an ideal bottler, or money-collector. During the war he played the syndicate, on the same bill as Vera Lynn and Wilson, Kepple and Betty. When there was no work, he played the streets. Although a natural comic, he has done a wide variety of acts. In 1949 he promoted himself and an antagonist as the first midget-wrestlers in England. He also did a high-diving act, diving forty feet into five feet of water. This act took him around the holiday resorts, such as Bournemouth, Rhyl, Blackpool, and Morecambe, and also to America. In 1948 he spent six months in America with the King Brothers' circus, playing in New York and Macon, Georgia. In 1954 he went back for four years. He worked in three different circuses, and toured twenty-eight states. He was with the King Brothers again for a time, and then worked in the Greatest Show on Earth, run by Ringman Brothers, Barnum and Bailey. Finally he worked for Clyde Beatty, but had to return to England when the authorities found that his three-month visa was expired. Since returning to England he has played in pantomimes like *The Best Years of Your Life*, and ice shows at the Empire Pool, Wembley. But he says he gets more of a kick out of playing on the streets. There are a few like him who know both sides of showbusiness, the boards and the streets. When we met him the film cartoon *Snow White and the Seven Dwarfs* was playing at a cinema in Haymarket, in the West End, and he was doing the queues with two musicians (*see* Plate 12). All the children loved him, dressed in his bright magenta and turquoise coat, with his way of getting them to guess which one of the dwarfs he is. He knows just how to get them to respond: 'I'm not Dopey, I'm not Bashful, I'm not Grumpy, I'm not Sneezy, I'm not Doc, I'm not Sleepy. Who am I then?' 'You're Happy,' they all shriek. And this is his life. He will continue to do parts in pantomime, or perhaps the occasional bit of film work, but it is the streets he loves best. It may not be a secure or lucrative existence, but for a performer like Roy it has its own rewards.

In September 1964 Angus McGill of the *Evening Standard* wrote an article focusing on two new faces on the London busking scene. Alan Young and Don Partridge were the first young street musicians to be seen in London since the war. Until they arrived there had only been the old regulars and disabled ex-servicemen. The new arrivals had been touring the seaside resorts as a duo of guitarists, and their arrival in London caused some excitement among those who had an interest in street life. Some saw them as a new generation of buskers to keep alive a tradition that seemed to be dying out as London began to swing to the sound of the Mersey beat. They found a London that welcomed the vitality they had to offer, and media that were ready to pick up on all the details. Don Partridge got himself into the newspapers as the Birdman of Ealing when he attempted to fly off Hammersmith Bridge using a pair of home-made wings. It was a publicity stunt, but no further attention was really needed from the press in those heady days. He and Alan used to promote concerts by fairly esoteric performers, like Jessie Fuller or Burt Jansch, and make a loss. They paid for the losses out of the money they made on the streets. They printed a Union of

Buskers and Street Players membership card which bore the following stringent set of rules:

1 There are no rules.
2 That all buskers be human.
3 That all buskers be capable of consuming 2 pints of beer in 1 minute.

Besides the union card, Alan also had a personal calling card, on which he described himself as a blues and folk guitarist singer, and 'Also Poet, Philosopher, Writer, Self-Styled Intellectual, Aimless Footed Drifter, and Late King of the Buskers'. On the reverse side of the card was a short poem:

What Is That   by A. Young

Are you what you do
Or what you feel
In essence which of you is real
Perhaps you think you are
And that is you
But who is what you really do?

Alan told us with a touch of irony that he had the cards printed in the days when he still thought he was a genius, a phase we all go through.

A slightly more serious project that he and Don attempted was to publish a book of their own poems and songs. In those days printing costs were low, and they financed the production of 1,000 copies themselves. These they tried to sell on the streets or in pubs. In a sense it was a revival of the old ballad-sheet tradition that had been strong until the nineteenth century. In 1967 something happened that helped them to sell out their first edition of poems completely. Don Partridge became a star. He appeared on *Top of the Pops*, the BBC's popular music programme with his song 'Rosie', and became the first one-man band to enter the Hit Parade. He suddenly found himself with a lot of money, fame, and a manager. The following year he formed a group, Don Partridge and the Wild Foul, which included Alan, and they played venues such as Blackpool Pier for three months. But it is not in a street musician's nature to be tied down to a commitment for very long, and the band split up. Alan found that as a one-man band, an image he had lent to Don, people kept coming up to him, banging the drum, and asking him to play 'Rosie', so he decided to change to solo guitar or banjo. In the meantime, Don was enjoying his newfound popularity. He bought a snake-skin jacket, and started to call himself 'Snake-hips Partridge, King of the Street-singers'. The climax of this honeymoon period came in 1969 with a concert at the Royal Albert Hall, organised by Partridge and his manager, Don Paul. It was something that had been talked about by Alan and Don before the success of 'Rosie', but had not been possible while they were just two relatively unknown street singers. The idea was to present a concert of buskers, drawing together the old, experienced figures with the new generation of street singers that had started with Alan and Don, and had increased in the subsequent four and a half years. So on 29 January 1969 there was very little music on the streets of London, but quite a lot in the Royal Albert Hall. The show was compered by 'Paris' Nat Scharfer, a former Hyde Park orator and street accordionist. Among the most popular of the old firm was Meg Aikman, a street singer who still performs unaccompanied in the streets of Soho, and occasionally makes guest appearances when London is visited by her more famous friends, Paul Simon and Art Garfunkel. The Road Stars made a special comeback, and Banjo and Spoons (*see* Plate 10) were also there. Another performer that night who is still going is Jumping Jack (*see* Plate 11), or the Earl of Mustard. He can still sometimes be found tap-dancing to the sound of a tape recorder outside Knightsbridge tube station. Others of the old firm have since disappeared from the streets. George Franks, the 62-year-old trumpeter, and leader of the Happy Wanderers jazz band, performed at the Royal Albert Hall, a venue to which he was by no means a stranger. Sadly, he can no longer play, for reasons of health. Tony Turco, an accordionist with thirty years of street experience behind him, was another who is no longer playing. Robert Malcolm, another fine accordion player and singer, had been on the streets for thirty-three years, starting when he was twelve. He had a clubfoot, which was partly why he became a street musician, and also partly why he drank. He used to get blind drunk, and often lost his accordion. Nine years after his performance at the Royal Albert Hall, he drank himself to death.

The younger generation were also represented at the busking concert. Alan Young, wearing a jester's cap and bells, read some of his poems as well as singing songs he had written himself, such as 'Ballad of London Town'. A one-man-band artist, known as Scotty to the busking fraternity, was another of those young men who have kept to the life of the streets and roads ever since. Of course, top of the bill was Don Partridge, with his two famous songs, 'Rosie' and 'Blue Eyes'. The event in a way confirmed the continuation of a tradition. Those who helped to organise it said that the street musicians were temperamental and well nigh impossible to manage. People who are used to total freedom do not like being told what to do or where to stand, and nervous tension ran high in the dress rehearsal. But the fact that Partridge managed to pull it off at least showed that the older buskers recognised him as of their kind.

The event may have been a statement about the regeneration of a tradition, but it also meant that busking had been commercialised. A long-playing record of the highlights of the concert was made, but most of the tracks were either mixed or over-dubbed in a studio, and some were actually re-recorded there. The essence of street music is not its technical perfection or its tonal quality, so much as its spontaneity and freedom, and to falsify the sound in a studio seems to be a contradiction of all its values.

A film was also made of the concert, and it was sold successfully all over the world. The men behind the organisation of the whole affair did pretty well out of it. For Don Partridge, it was more publicity, besides whatever percentage he may have taken. But for all the street entertainers who took part, there was not one penny. So for them, 30 January 1969 meant back to the winter streets to earn a living.

With the end of the 1960s, swinging London did not seem to swing so much. Britain's economy started to worsen, and the

Plate 10 (*above*) Banjo and Spoons, and bottler, London 1967
Plate 11 (*opposite*) The Earl of Mustard

only people with any money seemed to be tourists. For Alan Young the atmosphere was ripe for leaving, and in 1971 he set off with the ambition of busking round the world, taking his cap and bells with him. He saw himself as a sort of modern wandering troubadour, taking his own music with him as his only means of subsistence. He got as far as Yugoslavia before turning back to be with his wife at the birth of their first child. But he did not return to London to live. From 1971 until 1974 he was based in Copenhagen. The Danes did not have a busking scene as such. Their traditional *spielemen* used to visit country dances, weddings, and other celebrations, playing the violin to provide music for dancing. By 1971 they had been institutionalised, living on a state pension rather than contributions from the revellers, a sort of extension of the welfare state. Alan's activities aroused a certain amount of interest, and he found it possible to live there. After 1972 he made occasional visits to Stockholm to see Don Partridge. It was in that year that the *Daily Mail* had announced Partridge as 'The £50,000 overnight failure', as the one-time pop star was back on the streets busking for a living. Prudence is not one of the characteristics normally associated with those inclined towards the nomadic existence. Easy come, easy go is more in line with their life style, and they admit that it is so. Partridge continued to receive good offers from recording or other work, but disdained them all, preferring to strike out in his own direction.

Stockholm in the mid-seventies seemed to be the focus of attention for street musicians, and in 1974 Alan Young went there too. The Swedes had had their own tradition of itinerant musicians. Accordion players used to travel around and play, not in the streets, but in the courtyards of dwellings. But it had more or less died out in the 1940s. Alan soon met up with two other English buskers and a full-time bottler, and a successful band was the result. As they managed to stay together for some time, they were able to develop their act to include dance and mime. Whips formed a considerable part of the business. The loud crack drew the attention of the crowd, and cigarettes could be whipped from the mouths of bystanders. Or the handle could be used for a

Plate 12 (*opposite*) Roy, Alan and Scotty, London 1980

mock microphone. The group became a well-known part of the Stockholm scene, and eventually a thirty-minute film was made for television, based on their act and Don Partridge, with street shots, interviews, and comedy. It was called *Tjiboom Tjiboom*, and it made them famous throughout Sweden. The immediate result was that they earned more money on the streets, but after a while takings evened themselves out to normal again. The band was also asked to take part in a well-known television comedy show. The two comedians, comparable in reputation to Morecambe and Wise, were filmed busking in the streets. Alan dressed as a policeman, came along, moved them on, and then brought out his own band and banjo, and started to play in their place.

Although they were working the streets separately, Alan and Don did collaborate on the production of a second book of poems and songs while they were in Stockholm. So in 1977 *before and after* was published by Clandestine Publications, in a slightly glossier cover than the booklet of ten years before. Here is Alan Young's 'The Swans':

> green white and brown
>
> the fields, the river by the road
> the swans, the lorry and the load
> of feathers floating down
>
> screetch squawk and crash
> the brakes, the creatures desperate run
> the futile swerving body flung
> in fleshy metal smash
>
> run fly and keen
> the other bird will cry above
> the lover left to drift along
> a weeping willow stream.

There is a certain dignity of rhythm and economy of language about this that places it far above the standards of street-doggerel the cynical might have expected from a writer untrained in

Plate 13 A spontaneous collaboration; Alan Young and friend, London 1980

literary tradition. One might see it as a metaphor for the vulnerability of the simply natural and beautiful in a harsh technological age. Or perhaps it is just a sad song, simply expressed.

Back in London over the last two years, Alan has seen enough ups and downs to make him realistic about his life style. The TV and cabaret appearances come few and far enough between, and for the most part the streets are his livelihood. He sees it as a calling in a sense, a continual need to perform, while never wanting to be tied down. He also has a strong sense of the traditional aspect of his life, and sees himself as a descendant of the wandering minstrels and jongleurs. And, being a composer, he also claims the right to think of himself as a modern-day troubadour. He says that he gets a lot of respect from pop and folk singers because part of them wants to be there, on the streets. The street musician is at a middle point between the world of showbiz, the underworld, and the ordinary working people who pass him by every day, and if he keeps his eyes open a lot can be learned about people and life. He does not seem too concerned about what other people might consider to be lost opportunities to capitalise on a situation. He says: 'If you don't go into the mill of mass media, you've wasted yourself, so they say. If you live and die poor you've wasted yourself. But have you, by comparison with someone who's made a lot of money selling shoes? I prefer to live the life.'

It is impossible to make definitive statements about a busker, and say this is what he is doing Now. In October 1980, Alan Young was the man in the top hat in Plate 12, and was busking the cinema queues while Roy bottled. But unpredictability is part of a busker's psychological make-up, and by now he could be anywhere in Europe with his banjo, and his cap and bells, which he still wears occasionally.

The third member of the band in Plate 12 is Scotty. He was one of the younger generation of buskers at the Royal Albert Hall concert in 1969. When we asked whether or not the size of the auditorium overawed him that night, he told us it was nothing. Playing the streets is much more difficult, and takes a lot of nerve. He told us that a few years ago Steve Gibbons, a successful pop singer, was in London to record an album, and he got interested in Scotty's busking. He asked if he could join in the act, which at the time included another busker called Jake. So they agreed to play blues, but when Gibbons came to sing, he turned his back on the crowd because he could not stand the people looking at him. Scotty and Jake laughed at him, and told him to turn round or go away, but when he turned round, he still sang looking at the ground. He just could not bear to face his audience. And yet he could walk onto a stage in front of 5,000 or work in front of cameras without feeling self-conscious.

Like Alan and Roy, Scotty has had experience of working in the regular world of entertainment. A few years ago he worked with Ken Campbell, helping to write the Ken Campbell Road Show. Scotty had heard of an imaginary First World War hero called Sylvester McCoy, and he borrowed the idea to create a comical superhero for the show. The show ran at the Royal Court Theatre, and also toured the country. They stayed as guests of the Arts Council at Dartington Hall in Devon for four weeks, while the show toured in the South West. Scotty left the show, which subsequently went to America. A film was made of it, and excerpts were used in the successful satirical comedy show *The Secret Policeman's Ball*. Sylvester McCoy may not be as well-known as Superman, but his following is growing, and he is a frequent intruder in one of the country's most popular Saturday morning TV shows, *Tiswas*. A lot of money was made out of the venture, but hardly any of it found its way to Scotty.

Another brush with the other half occurred in 1976. Led Zeppelin, who at the time were probably the world's most popular rock band, were in London for the première of their film *The Song Remains the Same*, at a cinema in Leicester Square. Scotty was busking there, and Led Zeppelin's drummer, the late John Bonham, asked him to come to the party that evening, and to bring along some street characters. The inside of Floral Hall, Covent Garden, which had been hired for the event, seemed to have been turned into a mini-Soho. There were stalls for fruit, sea food, hamburgers, fish and chips, and of course drink. The buskers, who included Roy, were just told to do whatever they wanted. By 6.30 the following morning, most of the guests had collapsed *in situ*, but Scotty was still going strong. An hour and a half later he was at Trafalgar Square to do a short commercial film for Brazilian TV. They wanted a busker standing behind the sign for Trafalgar Square Underground station, advertising the kind of sights a Brazilian tourist might find in London. But the sign was too high, so they asked Scotty to stand on a box. Because of the previous night's heavy session, he kept falling off the box, and eventually they had to do the shot with two men holding his legs to prevent him from falling off, and him holding his stomach to prevent himself from ruining the take.

Like most full-time street musicians, Scotty does not like to stay in one place for too long. He likes to travel in France when London gets a bit dull. Busking in the Champs-Elysées in Paris can be more lucrative than any pitch in London, and also the police tolerate street music, unlike in England. The Cote d'Azur is also a favourite area for itinerant buskers. There is always a lot of money looking for something to be spent on, and, depending on luck as well as talent, a busker can do well. One summer, Scotty was asked by a rich English meat merchant to play at his private beach-café. It was a nude bathing beach, and Scotty said he found making the collection a bit disconcerting. He himself wore trunks and a vest, and also one knee-length riding boot which carried the hook and string necessary to bang the bass drum on his back.

Another time he and a group of other street musicians salvaged a boat that had sunk. The boat turned out to belong to the French singer Charles Aznavour. Aznavour's agent came down from Paris to survey the damage and take charge of the wreck, and when he found that it had been salvaged by buskers, he let them keep it. They fitted it out again, and about thirty people started to live on it. As the boats moored on either side were hardly ever in use, it was one virtually continual party until the police arrived, suspecting drug offences. No drugs were found, but one busker who had recently done well was fined for hoarding undeclared currency. The police came back the next day with frogmen and claimed to have found some illegal substances on the sea bed. All aboard were taken in for questioning, and although no prosecutions could possibly be made, the police used the opportunity to tow the boat to a breakers' yard, and smash it up. Life, for the street musician, is like that. One day he may be enjoying an easy life, and the next be back on the streets singing for enough money to buy a bite or a drink. And because he goes against the usual and expected patterns of social behaviour, he can expect no help at all from the authorities. Like Alan Young, Scotty is phlegmatic about his life's lack of security. He says that there is no such thing as security, that it is an illusion. He also says that one of the best feelings in the world is to sleep rough and to wake up without even enough money for breakfast. His music is more important to him than anything else. After singing all day to earn a living, he will drink until the pubs shut, and then sing and play for hours on into the night, just for the love of it, and still be back out on the streets again the next morning, no matter how cold, singing. A one-man band is not the sort of place one looks to find virtuosity, but he is an extremely fine guitarist and blues singer, and commands a lot of respect from musicians, street or otherwise.

Of course, the entire London busking scene does not revolve

around the group in Plate 12. Their combination, although it had the permanency of a mayfly, was a useful focus that showed the street tradition as an organic and living thing, passing its knowledge on from generation to generation. If the buskers are dying out, there are younger men to take their place.

One traditional aspect of street music that still lingers in London is the war invalid. He is somebody who has been around since before history began, and was certainly present at the start of our story. A fairly well-known team are Ernie and Jack. They are both disabled, and Jack bottles for Ernie, who plays the banjo outside tube stations. Ernie was in the army as a musician, and during the Second World War was a stretcher bearer. He was shot in the legs while rescuing a wounded man. In the thirty-five years since the end of the war he has busked in London regularly. He and Jack have a weekly pattern. On Mondays they are outside Green Park tube, on Tuesdays Bond Street, on Thursdays Sloane Square, and on Fridays Knightsbridge. They move around because if people saw them every day they would tire of making contributions. As it is, they have certain commuters who like to give regularly, once a week. In the days after the war when there were a lot more ex-servicemen playing the streets, they all used to meet on Sunday mornings in Petticoat Lane market. They would play all together, about thirty of them, playing military marches for a couple of hours, after which they would all go into the Bell public house and share out the takings. On those Sundays working partnerships were set up, and arrangements made to visit fairs and agricultural shows, or whatever suitable events were up and coming. Now there are so few ex-servicemen left that there are no more regular meetings. They finished about twelve years ago.

Ernie and Jack have both been in films. They featured in Ken Richardson's *Look Back in Anger*, as a bit of authentic local colour. They were also in a film about the porters at the old Covent Garden fruit market called *Every Day Except Christmas*, which won the 1967 Venice Film Festival award for documentaries. But this does not stop them from being harassed occasionally by the police. Sometimes they are told that busking is an offence in the Royal Borough of Kensington, but Ernie is sceptical. He reckons that some policemen may not always be telling the truth. He remembers being taken in by one constable who, on being asked what the charge was, replied that he would make one up as he went along. On the whole, though, he and Jack are accepted as part of the scene, and most policemen turn a blind eye to them, realising that they are not really any kind of nuisance. They busk all the year round, and although their takings make a small supplement to their war pensions, they carry on more for the enjoyment than the money. Ernie says: 'It's my life. I've always played music.' Being disabled, it is not easy to find suitable work, and they both prefer to be out among the crowds than shut up at home all day.

Having mentioned two old-time bottlers, it seems a good point at which to discuss the origin of this unusual term 'bottler'. It is supposed to originate from Bartholomew Fair, when street musicians needed somebody to collect money for them. Because it was unwise to trust anybody of casual

Plate 14 The One-Stringed Fiddler, London 1980

acquaintance, a busker would make his bottler hold a bluebottle in one hand, and the hat in the other. If the bluebottle was still in the bottler's hand at the end of a pitch, the busker knew that he could not have transferred any money from the hat into his own pockets, or otherwise the fly would have escaped. So from bluebottle we have the term 'bottler'.

Before the days of supermarkets and motorcars, whole communities used to come out and mix in the street markets, and of course the street musicians would be there too. Some of these markets still exist, although they are not as central to the life of ordinary people as they were. The Portobello Road market in London is famous, and attracts thousands of visitors every Saturday. Some come to buy antiques or curiosities, while others just come to look at the wares and feel the atmosphere. The more extrovert go to exhibit themselves, for it is a place to be seen, and a place full of genuine and phoney eccentrics. It is a place that attracts buskers, and the music, often coming from a source hidden by crowds, adds to the festive atmosphere. Some of the musicians are transient, but others are more regular visitors. The gentleman in Plate 14 has a certain dowdy sobriety as he sits there in his maroon bow-tie, playing his phonofiddle. He prefers to be known as the One-Stringed Fiddler, and has a long history of musical activity. He first played cornet in a military band when he was eight, following in his father's footsteps. He also learned to play the violin, but it was the phonofiddle that captured his imagination. Before the war it was played on stage as well as by buskers. He has nine instruments, most of which a friend made for him. The one in the picture is made from a cricket bat, his own idea, and has famous cricketer tea cards decorating it. He also had one with him that was made from a huge wooden spoon, and told us of one he had at home made from an old camping kettle and the sound-box of a mandolin. He used to make a living out of full-time street music, but now he does it only at weekends for the enjoyment. His material comes from what he called semi-classics, such as *The Merry Widow*. When we saw him he was playing 'Mull of Kintyre', Paul McCartney's popular song, and according to a nearby stallholder, had been playing it all morning.

Another old character whose appearance is striking is Walley. He comes from a tradition of itinerant showmen, as his mother was a fortune-teller in a travelling fair. Walley spent most of his life at sea, but has had about twelve years on the road with his grind-organ, a beautiful lacquered Victorian instrument. He is usually in Portobello Road on Saturdays, and during the week visits towns in the country. Sometimes he travels with Joey Stephens' fairs. His professional name is Theo R. Gangrinder, and his parrot, who dances on the revolving disc on the organ, is called Smarty. He finds the police in London fairly tolerant, although in the provinces they are less lenient, and he did tell us that he is 'the only busker to have been kissed by a copper'. He was once arrested by a young plainclothes policewoman who had been after the three-card-men, illegal street-gamblers, in the Bayswater Road. The WPC missed the card sharps, and picked Walley up instead on suspicion. He took his parrot with him to court, and was acquitted. After the hearing the policewoman came up to apologise for all the bother she had caused him with the arrest, and they got talking in quite a friendly way, so that when Walley went she gave him a goodbye kiss.

Walley has the true showman's instincts for public drama. On one of the occasions we met him, we were just approaching him when we heard a clamorous argument. A man in his thirties, with two young children, was denouncing Walley as not caring for him, his son, or for his grandchildren, and was making accusations about his behaviour with young ladies, and calling him a dirty old man. Walley responded by making equally rude references to his 'son's' private life, and the argument seemed to end in an irreversible rift in the family. It just left Walley placidly chuckling to himself, and he told me afterwards that they are not related, but were just putting on a bit of a show to pull a crowd. Walley gets a lot of children who like to play with Smarty, who will stand on a youthful head or a shoulder without biting if he is told to.

Bob, the blind accordion player (*see* Plate 15), has been on the streets for twenty-seven years, and is a regular figure in Portobello Road on Saturdays. He also busks in some West London pubs at weekends. Despite his blindness and generally poor appearance, he is cheerful and friendly. All the other regulars know him well, and he is never short of a friend to guide him to the pub or buy him a drink. He plays folk tunes and jigs and is a really good musician. Unfortunately, the standard of musicianship in Portobello Road does vary quite a bit. There are more guitars than anything else, as is the case everywhere now, and some of these are just casual visitors, hoping to pick up a bit of cash. Some can play well, but sometimes one comes across electric guitarists with battery-powered amplifiers, who only know a few rock-and-roll chords, bashing away at high volume. One also finds one or two devotees of that songwriter whose individual genius has given others a fifteen-year excuse not to sing in tune, Bob Dylan. However, economic factors discourage those who are more annoying than charming. Nobody gives them any money. Bob Dylan and rock-and-roll can be heard on the streets played well, but they are often what a beginner first learns to play, and, in places like Portobello Road especially, one sometimes gets beginners trying their luck.

Plate 15 Bob, the blind accordion player, London 1980

In the past ten years many groups have come into being, concerned at the demise of traditional communities and their natural cores, marketplaces. Pressure groups have managed to convince town planners that shopping centres with pedestrian precincts, and streets sealed off to motorised traffic, create healthier social atmospheres. These places are now regularly used by performing artists. Every university has its street theatre groups, who perform plays, songs, or general buffoonery, either to collect money for charity, or to make some political point. Feminist groups have their own street theatre. It is a valid way of awakening ordinary people's consciousnesses to ideas and currents in society that are important, but tend to get squashed as a minority voice. Drama and mime can be particularly effective, as they can be simple and forceful while being entertaining, and a bystander who is entertained is more likely to be sympathetic to the ideas being put over.

Other groups use the spaces for less politicised reasons. Morris-dancing is a popular pastime, and there are clubs all over the country. There are also street theatre groups who like to entertain, simply believing that the streets are there for the people to make of them what they will, rather than being regimented by traffic concerns and town planners. In the summer of 1978 a street theatre group called Ashes, otherwise Judy Boyle and David Mahon, arrived in London after performing successfully for years in Australia and New Zealand. They performed a show for children called *Willie the Clinket* in Rupert Street, Soho, and were arrested for obstruction. Their case was due before the magistrates at Bow Street that August and there were large demonstrations outside the courts on the day of the hearing. The hearing was put off for some legal reason, but a bigger demonstration was planned by another group, the Demolition Decorators, a demonstration for the right to perform on the streets. It took place on a warm Friday evening, 18 August 1978. A crowd of nearly a thousand gathered in Leicester Square to watch a performance of clowns, singing and dancing. There was nearly a riot when the police moved in to arrest the demonstrators. Nothing essential was changed by the demonstration. The police still have the right to remove anybody they consider to be obstructing the footpath, which they use at their own discretion. But the Demolition Decorators made their point, and drew attention to the issue. The media are now firmly on the side of street entertainment, and give it frequent coverage. One of the points being raised by supporters is that, as tourism is now one of Britain's biggest exports, it seems nonsensical to clamp down on any source of interest to visitors, especially one which the Tourist Board does not have to pay for.

Another area in which busking seems to be the victim of mean-minded bureaucracy for no good reason is the London Underground. Every station carries warnings that a busker is liable to a fine of £50 if caught. At Oxford Circus tube station, London Transport have even gone to the expense of installing a loudspeaker system that plays taped music as an alternative to the buskers. The commuters, for whose benefit the music has been laid on, tend to prefer the live performances. Article after article in the newspapers quoted commuters as saying that the busker in the tube is the only thing that can possibly brighten up going to work on a Monday morning. Other tube users feel compelled to write to the papers about the high standard of music that can be heard. The shaggy, be-denimed guitarist singing Bob Dylan songs may be the archetype of a busker in most people's minds, but there is in fact a great deal of variety, from classical to jazz, on offer under ground. Some buskers may be classical music students trying to augment their grant, but there are some who actually make their living playing in the tubes. The tube buskers are a slightly different set to the fresh-air buskers. The fresh-air buskers will say that they are the true street artists of traditional origin. The tube buskers are on average a bit younger than their fresh-air colleagues, and it is possible that the resurgence of buskers without a corresponding replacement of above-ground pitches has meant the creation of a whole new generation of underground buskers. They are certainly not tied to London. A duo of cello and flute, who play regularly at Charing Cross tube station, have travelled in Europe. They are both educated young men, who now live in a squat and live by music. Their middle-class families are a bit concerned about the future for them, but they say that while it works and is good, there is no reason to

stop. They play a high standard of baroque music that can sometimes earn them £10 an hour, but usually brings in less. The flautist, Vince, has played in Cambridge and York, Brussels, Munich, Freiburg, Berlin, most large towns in Switzerland, the South of France, Sienna, Florence, and Venice. He described his speedy exit from Italy:

> While busking in front of the Doge's Palace in Venice I felt a great sense of cultural victory over the tourist industry when a gondola drifted past with an accordion player singing watered-down Verdi to a couple of tourists in the front of the boat. A number of people listening to me turned round and told him to shut up, because they wanted to hear the flute playing. Ten minutes after this I was arrested and charged by a plainclothes Italian policeman (for vagrancy, which seemed a bit much) and given twenty-four hours to get out of the country, so I suppose they got their own back.

His partner, Nick, has not travelled so widely, but they are both in their early twenties yet.

We spoke to another duo at Leicester Square tube station, this time of flute and violin. The violinist, Michael, also lived in a squat, with his brother, a mandolin player, and several other buskers. His partner was German, and for him London was just a stage in a world tour. He had busked in America, where he found the police extremely intolerant. He had also been to Canada, but a street musician requires a licence that costs $500 a month, and he got deported for playing without one. He said that too much organisation takes the soul out of street music, and he prefers the freedom to move on when he feels like it. Most of the other buskers we spoke to were of the same opinion. To legalise busking would be a good thing, but to try to organise it would destroy the essence of its freedom. The German flautist's travels had taken him through South as well as North America, and he did admit that he had had to sell things to help finance his fares.

London is a stopping point for many international itinerants. The group in Plate 17 were German, and could speak very little

Plate 16 (*opposite*) Tube busker, London 1980

Plate 17 Band of foreign visitors, London 1980

English. They had made the Saturday trip to Portobello Road, but the rather timid way in which they huddled together, rather than playing out to the crowds, suggests that they were not very experienced in street playing, as a group at least. Another foreign visitor was a Spanish bagpiper. He also spoke no English, and we conversed in French. He was playing outside Selfridges in Oxford Street, having found getting a pitch in the tubes difficult with his language barrier. He described himself as a vagabond, and had made his way up from his home in Spain, through France, solely by playing his Galician bagpipes. He had been to Wales, and had slept rough on the road, in October. He said that he found smaller towns better because in the big cities people rush past without time to stop and listen. From England he hoped to travel through to Italy and then Yugoslavia.

Street musicians who travel in Europe find London a relatively hostile place. Other cities in other countries have central squares or piazzas where street entertainment is a recognised activity. A visit to the square outside the Centre Georges Pompidou in Paris is a completely different experience to a visit to Leicester Square. There it is like a continual circus. Mime artists, solo musicians, rock bands, and fire-eaters come, perform, and go (*see* Plates 18–24). Some are mediocre, but there is so much competition from high quality performers that the lack of an audience discourages them. The fakirs (Plates 20–22) went through an act that lasted about half an hour and included fire-eating, escaping from chains, and lying on broken glass. The shorter, dark-haired fakir was a good showman, and knew how to manage a crowd's interest. Although he shouted hoarsely in barely distinguishable French, we did not lose out on the tension he built up leading to the burst of flame from his friend's mouth. The electric street band (Plate 24) were also extremely good. When we arrived they were playing Santana's 'Samba Pa Ti', an instrumental popular in the early seventies, and their Latin American rhythm section fitted the sultry early evening atmosphere. It is true that in cold and rainy Britain some popular music fans would denounce such music as too 'laid back'. It belongs to a life style that one associates with California and beach parties, but it did not seem amiss in Paris. The French, as do most people from warmer parts of Europe, take sitting outside cafés in the streets for granted, rather than as a holiday treat, and it must colour their attitudes towards buskers. The police never interfere at the Pompidou, and it is accepted that musicians will play at all the little squares and cafés, not only in Paris, but in other towns in France. In Montpellier, for example, a fairly small university town in southern France, we saw in the course of three evenings, two jazz bands with full drum kits, mime artists, and solo saxophonist, numerous guitarists singing songs by the Beatles and the Rolling Stones, and a solo classical guitarist.

In Italy too the public square or piazza is still very much part of urban life. In Rome, the capital, there are not many buskers, because there are established café musicians, and also, if a group of young Romans cluster around a fountain or a statue, as they tend to do in the evenings, one of them is bound to have a guitar. But if anything goes on, it goes on at the Piazza Navona. The oblong piazza has been there since before the fall of Ancient Rome. It was originally the site of the mock sea-battles that were held at triumphs (*naves* is Latin for ships). It has now got cafés all along the sides, with tables outside. There are fire-eaters, street

Paris 1980
Plate 18 (*opposite top*) Classical guitarist entertains; Plate 19 (*opposite below*) Beautiful example of a barrel organ in pristine condition; Plate 20 (*above*) Fire holds no terror for the fakirs; Plate 21 (*left*) . . . nor does broken glass

Plate 22 (*above*) Just part of the build-up, outside the Centre Georges
Pompidou, Paris 1980
Plate 23 (*below*) The musical saw, Paris 1980

Plate 24 (*above*) Electric street band, Paris 1980
Plate 25 (*below*) Beautiful baroque music in the Piazza Navona

Plate 26 The youngest yet

artists, and jewellery-sellers, and also probably the youngest busker we have seen (Plate 26). The recorder player in Plate 25 was playing brilliant, sensitive baroque music, and had gathered an appreciative crowd when the little boy, no more than eleven years old, came along and sat quite close to him. He played the accordion well for his age, but only very simply. Unfortunately, he was much louder than the recorder player, who was drowned out and found the only way he could possibly be heard was to improvise in the same key as the accordion. After about ten minutes of improvising over the same four-chord sequence, the recorder player got fed up, and packed up and left. Quite soon afterwards the troupe of street actors in Plate 27 burst into the square, all singing a song with an infectious rhythm. They dragged their hand-cart around two sides of the piazza, and then set it up as a stage. They performed folk stories in mime, and also an act in which one of them lay on a bed of nails. Although they spoke Dutch, it did not prevent us, English or Italian, from being well entertained. When the act was over the police came up and asked a few questions, but there was no sense of pressure, and no action taken. They were a Dutch group who play on the streets and in small theatres in their own country, and they were taking a sort of working holiday.

One might ask the question why London has no central space for such people to play in. The reply might come back that it has, in the newly opened Covent Garden piazza, where buskers can be seen at all hours of the day. The truth behind this is that any busker who wants to play at Covent Garden must pass an audition with the Greater London Council, and is allowed a maximum of three hours a week. The GLC were worried that

Plate 27 Troupe of Dutch exhibitionists, Rome 1980

their new showcase for expensive shops would become infested by hordes of second-rate buskers, so they decided to control exactly what goes on. But if they had let it find its natural level, it is possible that the creation of a new and prestigious venue would have caused a high quality of competition, as at the Pompidou. An ignored busker soon gives up, and Covent Garden could have attracted enough talent to keep the standard high. As it is, some buskers disdain to audition for something that denies the essence of a street musician's life, freedom to move on when and where he or she chooses. Those who do play there admit that it is not really busking, so much as performing outside. The whole atmosphere is plastic and artificial, rather like a film set. The attitude of the authorities towards genuine street music is illustrated by an incident that occurred one Friday night a month or two after the opening. A roar of applause attracted our attention, but the first thing we saw was a security guard speaking into his walkie-talkie, and striding purposefully off in the direction of the uproar. The noise had been for a young man, of perfectly respectable appearance, who, inspired by the wine, the fine autumn evening, and perhaps some other motive, had risen to his feet to sing 'Daddy, Don't Go Down the Mine'. By the end of the first verse, all eyes were on him, and there were at least three security guards hovering just behind his back, looking as if they were about to set on him. He sang in an articulate and extremely well-modulated voice, and was appreciated by the audience, mainly of passers-by. The security guards looked extremely angry, but did not dare interrupt the performance, because several hundred people were enjoying it. Although they did not do anything, their presence was a nasty stain on the atmosphere that had been created by a bit of harmless fun.

It is a pity that the opportunity was not taken to give London its Centre Georges Pompidou. There is a lot of talent still in the streets of London, even if it is restricted to certain roads at certain times, or pushed into the tubes. There is a human type that will not be put off by fines for obstruction, or by voices telling it to get a sensible job and be some use to society. Buskers are some use to society, even if not in an economic sense. Regular arts, music, theatre, and painting also contribute little to the Gross Domestic Product, except perhaps as exports, but they are no less an important part of life. The busker is important, not merely because he brings us music on our way to work, but also because he represents the unpredictability and freedom that have been lost in most people's regimented lives. The footloose musician has always been around and his different perspective on life can give a fresh point of view to that coming from masses of people all trained to think the same way. He is society's joker, and like the Fool in *King Lear*, is destined to be kicked around by everybody while showing more insight than most. People ought to listen more to his point of view. It is apt to end with Alan Young's 'Free Bird Song':

> A bird sang in the forest
> And flew from tree to tree
> Careless songs of nothing
> High and low and free
>
> Over hills and down by streams
> And following the breeze
> In summer he would warm himself
> In winter he would freeze
> But as the seasons come and go
> And the songs went high and low
> He sang them as he pleased.

ACKNOWLEDGEMENTS

The authors gratefully acknowledge the co-operation of all who have helped in the development of this book. In particular we thank: Gary Williams, John Denny, Bill Coumbe, Janet Cohen, Frank Greenwood, Anne Ridley, David Hÿtch, Professor R. M. Ogilvie and Dr A. S. Gratwick of the Dept of Humanities, St Salvator's College, St Andrews, Julia Collieu, Elaine Farr, Giulio Somma, Ralph Hyde, the staff at The British Library, Chris Ridley, Tim Roney, Jim Forrest, 'Mike' Ridge and Margaret Kingham.

For permissions and services connected with illustrations, we thank: The Spurgeon Collection, Greenwich Libraries and The Guildhall Library, City of London for Plate 3; BBC Hulton Picture Library and The Guildhall Library for Plates 7, 8 and 9; The Guildhall Library for Figures 4 and 9; The British Library for Plates 4, 5, 6 and Figures 2, 6, 7, 8, 10, 11, 12, 13, 14, 15, 16, 17, 18 and 20; Leicestershire Museums, Art Galleries and Records Services for Plate 2; Centaur Press Ltd, Reginald Scot, for Figure 6 from *The Discoverie of Witchcraft*; George G. Harrap and Company Ltd for Figures 5 and 7 from *The Italian Comedy* by P. L. Duchartre; Punch Publications Ltd for Figure 19; Merlin Photographic, Musselburgh, Midlothian and David C. L. Stock for Plates 10 and 11; S. Charitonidis, L. Kahil and R. Ginouvès for Plate 1.

Figures 1 and 3 by Anne Ridley; Plates 12–27 by Ben Greenwood.

We also thank Frank Cass and Company Ltd for advice on *London Labour and the London Poor* by H. Mayhew; and Paddington Press Ltd for extracts from *The Women Troubadours* by Meg Bogin.

Finally, but by no means least, we have spoken to a number of buskers; we are grateful to them for their help and guidance, in particular Vince, Nick, Walley, Alan, Scotty and Roy.

BIBLIOGRAPHY

Alexander, Michael (translator), *The Earliest English Poems* (1966, second edition 1977); a collection of Old English poetry translated into modern English, with useful introduction and extensive notes.

Aydelotte, Frank, *Elizabethan Rogues and Vagabonds* (1913); a fascinating study of the Elizabethan underworld.

Babbage, Charles, *Passages from the Life of a Philosopher* (1864): 'A Short Chapter on Street Nuisances'; the author's own experiences of persecution by persistent street musicians, written in a tone of self-righteous indignation that becomes unintentionally humorous.

Bass, Michael Thomas, MP, *Street Music in the Metropolis* (1864); a collection of letters, press, and police reports published as part of a campaign to ban street music.

Bogin, Meg, *The Women Troubadours* (1976); valuable information on twelfth- and thirteenth-century Provençal women poets, but a confused thesis.

Bradbrook, Muriel Clara, *The Rise of the Common Player* (1962); a fairly specialised work on the factors leading to the establishment of professional theatre companies in the sixteenth century.

Breul, K. (editor), *The Cambridge Songs* (1926); a collection of Latin songs by itinerant scholars.

Briffault, Robert S., *The Troubadours* (Bloomington, Indiana, 1965); comprehensive work about the troubadour tradition, its Moorish origins, and its continuation in Europe after its decline in southern France.

Burch, Clive Edward Creed, *Minstrels and Players in Southampton 1428–1635* (Southampton 1969); a factual pamphlet containing records of the visits of travelling troupes to Southampton.

Carcopino, Jerome Ernest Joseph, *Daily Life in Ancient Rome*, translated by E. O. Lorimer (1956); an easily digestible background work.

Catullus, *The Poems of Catullus*, translated by James Michie (1969); an entertaining, modern, verse translation.

Chambers, Sir Edmund Kerchever, *The Elizabethan Stage* (1923); extremely detailed study of factors and individuals involved in the development of a professional theatre culture in Elizabethan England.

—, *The Medieval Stage* (1903); deals with all aspects of drama, religious plays, pagan folk myths, itinerant minstrels and players, etc from the Dark Ages through to the sixteenth century. Essential.

Charitonides, S., Kahil, L., Ginouvès, R., *Les Mosaïques de la maison de Ménandre à Mytilène* (Bern 1970); A well-illustrated archaeological work, concentrating on the house of Menander, with colour plates of mosaics.

Chaytour, Henry John, *The Troubadours* (1912); an interesting but imprecise account of the troubadours of southern France.

City of London Guildhall Library Prints Department; an extensive collection of notes, engravings, newspaper cuttings and photographs, concerning street life in London from the sixteenth century onwards.

Coryat, Thomas, *Coryat's Crudities* (1611); a travel book by a genuine eccentric, recounting experiences in Europe in the classic style of the Renaissance pedant.

Deloney, Thomas, *Works*, edited by F. O. Mann (1912); the collected works of an Elizabethan ballad singer, pamphleteer, and novelist.

Duchartre, Pierre Louis, *The Italian Comedy*, translated by Randolph Weaver (1929); the complete story of the origins, development, and eventual establishment in France of the Italian *commedia dell'arte*. More enthusiastic than accurate.

Farnell, Ida, *The Lives of the Troubadours* (1896); translation of biographies of many lesser, as well as the better-known troubadours, originally written by Uc de St-Cyr, himself a troubadour.

Goldoni, Carlo, *Memoirs*, translated by John Black (1926); the memoirs of one of Italy's greatest comic playwrights.

Hawkins, Sir John, *A General History of the Science and Practice of Music* (1875); a huge work tracing the history of music from earliest times, that unfortunately lacks any key to its contents.

Head, Richard, *The Canting Academy* (1674); a collection of songs and prose by and about sixteenth- and seventeenth-century vagabonds.

Hill, R. T. and Bergin, Thomas G., *Anthology of the Provençal Troubadours* (New Haven 1941); a collection of troubadour poetry, with prose translation, and instructive notes on the authors.

Hone, William, *The Everyday Book* (1831); a scrapbook telling the historical and traditional significances of every important day in the year. It collects some useful information about folk traditions that have since died out.

Horatius, Quintus Flaccus, *Works*; satires and epistles give a living picture of Ancient Rome.

Hueffer, Francis, *The Troubadours* (1878); more romantic than factual, but deals with roughly the same material as Chaytour.

Jonson, Ben, *Bartholomew Fair* (1614); Jonson's knowledge of London at street level comes across well in one of his best-loved plays.

—, *Volpone* (1605); includes a scene accurately presenting a mountebank.

Jusserand, Jean Adrien Antoine Jules, *English Wayfaring Life in the Middle Ages* (1961); a useful background to our work, also branching out into the world of pilgrimages and religious mendicancy.

Kemp, William, *Kemp's Nine Daie Wonder*, edited by Alexander Dyce (1840); the Elizabethan clown's own story of his dance from London to Norwich.

Livius, Titus, *History of Rome*; includes early origins of drama and music in theatres or out in the open.

Lucian, *De Saltatio*; mythical and historical origins of dance and mime, and their place in urban Roman society.

Martial, *Epigrams*; give insight into life in Ancient Rome.

Mayhew, Henry, *London Labour and the London Poor* (1864); the major Victorian work of sociology, including extensive interviews with street performers.

Morley, Henry, *Memoirs of Bartholomew Fair* (1859); a comprehensive history of the fair from its founding in the twelfth century.

Oliphant, Mrs M. O. and Tarver, F. B. C., *Molière* (1879); a short biography of France's great comic playwright.

Percy, Thomas, Bishop of Dromore, *Reliques of Ancient Poetry* (1765); includes an essay on minstrelsy that can be used with caution as to its historical accuracy.

Ribton-Turner, Charles James, *A History of Vagrants and Vagrancy* (1887); deals mainly with the Tudor problems with vagabonds.

Ritson, Joseph, *Ancient Songs and Ballads from the Reign of King Henry II to the Revolution* (1829); a large collection of English songs, mainly anonymous.

Schofield, Bertram (translator), 'The adventures of an English minstrel and his varlet' (1384), in *Musical Quarterly* Volume 35, (1949); the varlet's own confession to a French court of his intrigues in the politics of the time.

Scot, Reginald, *The Discoverie of Witchcraft* (1584); a huge work laying bare all the secrets of witchery, conjuring, juggling, etc practised in the sixteenth century.

Sims, George Robert, *Living London* (1903–5); a magazine with photographs, covering a variety of aspects of Edwardian London.

Smith, John Thomas, *Vagabondiana* (1817); observations of London street characters of the Napoleonic era, with engravings.

Smith, Sir Sydney Armitage (editor), *John of Gaunt's Register* (1911); John of Gaunt's letters of administration collected in no apparent useful order.

Smith, Sir William, *A Dictionary of Greek and Roman Antiquities* (Boston, Massachusetts, 1870).

Stow, John, *A Survey of London*, introduced by C. L. Kingsford (1908); a sixteenth-century attempt to compile a history of London from the sources available at the time.

Stubbes, Phillip, *An Anatomy of Abuses in England in Shakespere's Youth*, edited by F. J. Furnivall (1877–9); a collection of Tudor wickedness by one who disapproved.

Suetonius, Tranquilius, *The Twelve Caesars.*

Taylor, Hobart C. C., *Molière: a biography* (1907); larger than Mrs Oliphant's, but the same story.

Thomas, J. and Smith, A., *Street Life in London* (1877); with photographs.

Timbs, John, *The Romance of London* (1865); a loose collection of anecdotes and newspaper cuttings concerning London.

—, *Walks and Talks about London* (1865); more of the same.

Waddell, Helen, *The Wandering Scholars* (1927), scholarly work on Latin poets and scholars of the Dark Ages and early Middle Ages.

Welfitt, William, *Minutes from Ancient Records in Canterbury* (1802); a collection of old records without apparent theme or order.

Wille, Günther, *Musica Romana* (Amsterdam 1967); unfortunately there is not yet a translation of this large book, dealing with all aspects of music in Ancient Rome.

Wilshere, Jonathan E. O., *Leicester Towne Waytes* (Leicester 1970); a concise but factual pamphlet using old records about the development of the Leicester town band.

Wright, Thomas (editor), *Political Poems and Songs Related to English History Composed During the Period from the Accession of Edward III to that of Richard III* (1859); with notes.

—, *Songs and Ballads, with Other Short Poems, Chiefly of the Reign of Philip and Mary* (1860).

INDEX